THE TONBRIDGE OUTRAGE

A GRUESOME MURDER THAT SHOCKED EDWARDIAN SOCIETY

John Brookland

BITZABOOKS

First published in UK 2024
By Bitzabooks.co.uk
info@bitzabooks.co.uk

© John Brookland, 2024
ISBN: 978-1-0686450-1-3

Available as an ebook: ISBN: 978-1-0686450-0-6

All the characters are real, and no invented persons or storylines
have been included, but some of the dialogue and scenes have
been dramatized.

Verses in chapter headings are from the Broadside Ballad:
Tonbridge Murder and Outrage by James Lauri.
Cover by Bitza Books

Listen, old and young as well, a story I will tell,
Near Tonbridge there was done a dreadful deed,
It was on New Year's Eve, we have reason to believe,
A little girl was murdered, So we read….

THE CHILD'S FATAL ERRAND.

Illustrated Police News/British Newspaper Archive

In Memory Of
Frances Eliza O'Rourke
1894-1901

The Edwardian Detective Edwin Fowle Series

The Tonbridge Outrage
The Tenterden Murder
The Sevenoaks Tragedy
Casebook of an Edwardian Detective

Find other books by John Brookland on the
Amazon.co.uk bookstore.

CONTENTS

PROLOGUE

As dusk descended on New Year's Eve 1901 in the quiet village of Southborough in the County of Kent, England, the nineteen hundred residents were all in good spirits, eagerly anticipating celebrating the arrival of 1902. Not a single soul could have imagined that a fiendish and revolting rape and murder of a local seven-year-old girl was about to occur and disrupt their lives for the next three months. The "outrage" as it was referred to, shocked Edwardian society and caused fear and disquiet throughout the district, attracted national and international press coverage and the unwelcome morbid attention of thousands of sightseers.

Few residents were to remain untouched by it in the close-knit community. The Coroner described it as 'diabolical and gruesome, a crime so cruel in its inception and so repulsive in the details of its execution;' the trial Judge defined it as 'the most savage and cruel murder within my experience.' Although infanticide and rape of children was not uncommon, the horrific way the child was killed, and the body disposed of, made the incident more monstrous and notorious.

At the time of the murder Southborough was a small picturesque and thriving community perched on a hill overlooking steep wooded slopes of the North Weald. It is sandwiched between the famous major spa town of Tunbridge Wells two miles to the south and the town of Tonbridge three miles to the north. It's only claim to fame was for being a centre for manufacturing cricket balls, a game that had been played on its seventy-acre common since 1794. Most of its inhabitants were employed in agriculture and it had a busy livestock market.

The murder took place just north of the village in a byway named Vauxhall Lane, one of the most unfrequented areas in the district with the Vauxhall Inn public house at the top end and just a couple of farms laid back from the road along the rest of its two-mile length. After dark it was a very foreboding area and to this day remains a grim place at night.

The police were under pressure from the beginning to solve the crime quickly but were hampered by the lack of the technological and forensic assets that modern policing enjoy. It was early days in the investigation of crime and with the exception of Scotland Yard in London most police forces had no specialised detective departments until the late 1800s. The science of forensics was basic at best and of little help to them. Finger printing was only just being trialled in some cities, CCTV and DNA testing was nearly a century in the future. There was not even a test to distinguish between human and animal blood. There was no thought of approaching a crime scene "using the path of least common approach" or "bagging evidence" in order to preserve it. Therefore, most convictions were gained by collecting circumstantial evidence and this lack of corroborative forensics led to many accused persons being wrongly convicted on just witness testimony. The legal process was also convoluted with inquest and investigative magistrate hearings, grand juries and assize courts.

At the time the availability of adequate communication and transport was also an issue. The only means of distance transport available was by horseback, train or hired cab and there were only twenty police bicycles available in the County of Kent, so officers completed their beat on foot. With few telephone lines installed, messages were conveyed by telegram, post or runner. So, when solving serious crime, the police were always handicapped.

It was in this context that Superintendent Robert Styles, head of the Tonbridge Division, Kent County Constabulary was faced in solving the murder. It was protocol for the County Divisional superintendents to immediately refer high profile complex cases requiring specialist investigation to Kent's fledgling detective department in Maidstone and this is exactly what Styles did. It had only been operating since 1896 and its officers were still on a learning curve in detection methods and procedures. The unit consisted of just a sergeant and three constables responsible for the whole County and was the equivalent of the modern Flying Squad or Sweeney.

Heading the department was a much respected and renowned newly promoted officer in the form of First-Class Detective Sergeant Edwin Fowle. He had only been in charge for a year and suddenly found himself lead investigator in his first high profile murder case. He had a natural aptitude for detective work, was always smartly dressed and wearing a derby hat; a stickler for correct police procedure he was to have an unrivalled record of success as a detective.

This true story recounts his investigation of this ghastly murder of Frances Eliza O'Rourke. All the characters are real, and no invented persons or storylines have been included as the fascinating details of this factual story renders this unnecessary, but some of the dialogue and scenes have been fictionalised.

1.
New Year's Eve 1901

Frances Eliza O'Rourke, familiarly known as Fran was seven and a half years old going on ten, a vivacious and popular young girl described by her parents as of a bright and happy disposition, willing and useful in the house and their right hand. Her proud parents adored her. At about 2pm on New Year's Eve 1901 she was standing in front of the mirror in the hallway of her parent's house at 15 Elm Road, in the village of Southborough. She was adjusting her attire in readiness to run an errand for her father. She lived in a hectic household with her three younger sisters, Maudie, Nellie and Bertha, a new arrival only six months old. As usual she had helped her mother, who was also called Frances, organise breakfast and to wash and dress her other two sisters while her mother had devoted her energies to feeding and caring for baby Bertha. Being the eldest, Frances had gladly taken on the role of helping with her sisters and household chores. She was a good girl and had helped tidy and clean the house before preparing lunch and was now looking forward to her trip out.

Her father was thirty-year-old John Lancy O'Rourke a journeyman tailor by trade who worked from home. At lunch he had asked her to deliver a parcel containing trousers he had shortened for Jenkinson & Sons; an outfitters shop in Tunbridge Wells where he had been employed for many years. Fran loved helping her father and on these trips she liked to look her best and grown up. She had dressed in her distinctive new bright white straw boater with a black band which she had received for Christmas and was making sure it was sitting straight. She was proud of her wardrobe which that day included a brown checked ulster jacket over a blue serge frock, and she had wrapped a white neckerchief around her neck for added fashion. She wore black stockings, and her brown boots were clean. She was also proud of her long dark tresses that hung down her back. She stood back to admire herself and thought she looked rather stylish. Although not freezing cold it was still a chilly day and she wanted to keep warm. She was quite a tall girl, and her parents often told her she looked two or three years older which pleased her as she liked the idea of this. Having satisfied herself that her attire was perfect she went in search of her father. She walked into the back parlour and found him sitting at the table busily stitching.

'There you are Fran, I was wondering where you were,' said her father indulgently.

'Sorry, Papa, I was making sure my new boater looked smart.'

'You look very pretty in it my dear. Suits you. Now the package I want you to take to Mr Jenkinson is on the sideboard and here is a bill for six shillings he owes me. Make sure you give it to him.'

'I will.'

Fran picked up the brown paper parcel tied with string, 'What is in the parcel?' she asked.

'There are two trousers; a blue serge and a black pair with stripes which I have taken up. Whatever you do don't drop them in a puddle and get them wet.'

'Of course not Papa.' Fran gave a sigh as she had always been very diligent on past occasions without any mishaps. She had taken and collected packages to the shop since early August and enjoyed doing it. She liked Mr Bourdain the foreman cutter as he was kind to her.

'Can I have a ha'penny to buy some sweets please?' She asked using one of her most charming smiles.

'Sorry Fran I don't think I have a ha'pence.'

'Oh, please,' she tried again.

'I have a farthing, which will have to do my girl,' he said handing over the coin with another indulgent smile.

'Thank you Papa.'

'What is the time Fran?'

'It is twenty past two.'

'Well, you better get a hurry on. No dawdling either, as I want you back before dark as being New Year's Eve it's not a night to be out late,' added her mother from the scullery door.

'Yes, Mama,' she sighed again.

John took her to the front door and watched with a smile as she skipped up the road. He was devoted to her and trusted her as she was a bright and intelligent girl. She seemed so lively and happy as she disappeared down the street.

'Get back as soon as you can,' he shouted and closed the front door.

She liked to day dream while walking into town and to window shop particularly at the ladieswear shops. She hoped one day to be able to afford the long dresses, cloaks and furs and smart hats that she admired on the ladies that walked by her. She stood and watched a carriage pass by driven by a man in uniform with a footman. She waved to a lady in a hat peering out the carriage window at her who smiled and waved back. Perhaps that might be me one day she thought once I have married a rich young man. She hurried on. It was about an hour's walk to the tailors shop which she never found a problem, but she did want to get back quickly as being New Year's eve the family were having a special meal later. She made it to the shop in good time arriving at about 3.20pm and was greeted by Phillip Bourdain.

'Hello Frances, I see you have brought our parcel. How are you?'

'Fine, Sir,'

'And your father and mother?

'They are well too.'

'That's good.'

Fran gave Phillip her father's note. She often spent time talking to the staff about school and other things and looking round, but on this occasion she didn't stay too long as they were busy so after twenty minutes or so she informed Phillip she was going home.

He asked, 'Now I want you to do a favour for me Frances and take this pair of Eton trousers to your father. I have parcelled it up with a note inside. Is that alright?'

'Yes, sir. I'll look after it.'

'I'm sure you will. Thank you Frances,' he said handing her the small parcel in a black wrapper commonly used by tailors.

'See you next time and Happy New Year.'

'Thank you Mr Bourdain, and Happy New Year to you,' replied Fran leaving the shop.

'Such a polite girl he muttered,' as he returned to his cutting.

It was about ten minutes to four when she headed for home and the sun was low in the sky and already getting dark. She quickened her pace as it had started to rain. She spotted some girls she knew on the other side of the road and had a quick chat to one of them but was in too much of a hurry to linger. Half way home she was aware that a horse and cart was keeping pace with her, and she turned to look at it. A young man was driving and was looking over at her with a smile. He called over to her, but at first she ignored him and continued walking. He called out again, but she couldn't hear what he was saying so she stopped. She vaguely recognised him, but there were so many carters that used the road. The cart pulled up and the man asked her if she wanted a lift. At first she declined as she didn't normally accept rides but then thinking she needed to get

7

home quickly and the driver seemed a nice lad, she accepted the offer. She walked across the road and tried to climb up, but the step was high, and she struggled, so the man took her hand and pulled her up.

*

Twenty-year-old Harold Apted sat at the breakfast table at 69 Woodside Road, Tonbridge opposite his elderly father Thomas while his mother Ellen busied herself cooking. He listened to his father's laboured breathing. He wasn't a well man. He had been a hard worker for too many years, first on the land, then as a builder and finally setting up a small coal merchant business hauling coal, coke and faggots of wood. He had been forced to in order to support the family that never seemed to stop growing. Harold was the last of six brothers and five sisters that arrived over a period of twenty-five years. No wonder his mother looked so worn out. He loved his mother and smiled at her as she placed a plate of bacon and eggs in front of him.

Most of his siblings had now flown the nest, got married and moved out from what had been a noisy hectic household. Now it was just Harold and his 23-year-old brother Charlie at home, but his married brother John lived a few doors down the road at number 33. Charlie had already left for work. He was lucky. He had a job as a cricket ball maker with Mr Cockerill next door who had a small workshop. It was a thriving industry in town. In fact, all his brothers had done well, finding apprenticeships and becoming plumbers, builders, gas fitters and working on the railway which he resented to a certain degree.

Harold had tried to emulate his brothers. When thirteen he had got a job in a machine shop in the High Street and stayed there for a few years but couldn't settle down to it so in 1895 aged seventeen he got a job with Mr Hall the cycle and motor maker and was soon entrusted with renting out the cycles. He had enjoyed his work but one day after a heavy snowfall he had thrown snowballs at his fellow workers, and they complained to the boss. It wasn't the first time he had been warned about his bad behaviour and so he was sacked. He didn't argue over it as he didn't like the job that much. That was February 1897. His parents were not happy with his conduct, and he had a telling off from his father. His parents were religious and the family well respected in the area and they had made sure their youngest son had grown up as a regular church goer. Most people who knew him regarded him as a quiet, inoffensive and respectable young fellow. In fact, Harold had been a member of the Church Lads Brigade, a chorister and regular of Miss Warner's Bible class, something Ellen was proud of. She loved her son. But Harold was a bit of a rebel at heart, always well behaved in company so everyone who knew him had little idea of his true character. But now he was stuck at home, beholden to his father and forced to help carry on the family business. He wasn't entirely satisfied with his life. Harold finished his breakfast and put on his coat and cloth cap over his dark suit and pair of brown leggings.

Being New Year's Eve, he was looking forward to finishing work and having a celebratory drink with his new girlfriend named May to end the day. It would only be their third date and she was a "looker" and he was already keen on her. He knew it was going to be a long day as Tuesdays were always busy. He had tried to diversify his work whenever possible and had contracts with local farmers and slaughterhouses to deliver calves and livestock they had acquired at the Tuesday Tonbridge market.

'I'm off now,' he said to his parents.

His father looked up and asked, 'Have you got much on at the market?'

'Yes Dad, seven or eight calves to drop off to Mr Semple's and another slaughterhouse.'

'Drive careful son, and don't push that poor horse too hard. He's too old now.'

'Yes Dad.'

Their cart horse was a very old chestnut and should have been retired long before, but they couldn't afford to get a new younger one. The same could be said for their cart which had also seen better days. Harold had converted it with side boards when he began transporting livestock to keep them in and strengthened the floor with planks as well. He would carry any cargo he could get hold of and often moved furniture and other goods.

The family rented a stable and yard from George Gilham a furniture upholsterer who had a workshop in Priory Street at the junction with Pembury Road just a ten-minute walk away. It was part of Gilham's business premises. Harold unlocked the gate and went into the stable, greeting the horse who gave him a mournful snort in return. He owned one of the popular small four-wheeled open carts pulled by one horse, not one of the large waggons which needed at least two horses. He hitched the horse and headed at a gentle trot to the cattle market in Bank Street below the castle. He chatted to other carters and farmers that he knew and watched the livestock being auctioned. He loved the market banter and the busy and noisy atmosphere of the place.

Once the auction had ended, Phillip Emery who knew Harold, offered to help him load the seven calves he had been hired to transport. One of them had a leader rope on him and Harold dragged the indignant howling calf to the cart with the others following along. Phillip jumped up onto the cart and Harold lifted them up to him one by one. The last one to be loaded had the long rope attached and Harold didn't want it to tangle so he retrieved his knife from his pocket and cut it off. He then jumped up onto the seat, said thanks and goodbye to Phillip and headed down the main road that led from Tonbridge down to Southborough heading for the slaughterhouse belonging to Mr Semple. It took him nearly an hour, but he wasn't in a hurry. He offloaded three of the calves with the help of Frank Kemp who worked there. It was now lunchtime.

Frank was at a loose end with nothing more to do until later so at the suggestion of Harold he said he would accompany him to the Black Horse pub in Camden Road for a drink. So, they trotted through the town over Grosvenor bridge and down Quarry Road reaching the pub about 3pm with the remaining calves still in the back. Harold was in a good mood and the two had a good old natter while Harold downed "two-twos" of whisky, and they came out of the pub just before 4pm. Frank said he would walk back, and Harold climbed up and feeling relaxed decided he fancied another drink. So, he continued on to Forest Road and pulled up outside the Spread-Eagle pub just after 4pm. Having tied up the horse he went in and was just about to order another whiskey when another friend of his named Arthur Webb entered the bar. Arthur was also a carter and had seen his cart outside and spotted the calves in the back. He was with his father and the two of them wondered what Harold was up to and on entering spotted him ordering a drink at the bar. Harold saw Arthur and his father and called out, 'What are you doing here?'

'We saw the calves in the cart outside and wondered what you were up to,' Arthur replied.

'Having a drink what else. Fancy joining me?'

Arthur answered, 'Well as you're offering we'll both have a rum,'

The three of them chatted and then Arthur, who could see that Harold was getting a little merry, said, 'Who are those calves for?'

'They're for John Priestly the butcher in Calverley road,'

11

Arthur was worried about the well-being of the calves, so he said, 'don't you think he'll be wondering where they are by now?'

'I reckon,' responded Harold disinterestedly.

'Tell you what, how about us doing you a favour by driving them up there for you?'

At this point Harold started to sing and Arthur had difficulty getting his attention again.

'It's only a half mile from here. I'll be back before you know it.'

'Why not. I wish you would,' Harold answered mid song.

So, Arthur and his father left Harold singing while they took the calves to Priestly, a master butcher who owned a shop at 25 Calverley Road. When they returned Harold was still singing and greeted them loudly saying to Arthur, 'Now you're back I'll sing you another song.'

Arthur described Harold as being a "bit lively" at this point and they persuaded him to leave and all three jumped onto Harold's cart. Arthur and his father asked to be dropped off by St. Peters Church in Bayhall Road where Arthur noticed the clock showed 4.30pm. Then Harold headed back to Southborough as the light faded along Calverley Road and St John's Road. It was now raining but Harold in his open cart wasn't bothered and carried on as he was enjoying his afternoon drinking session. As he neared the stables he went into the British Volunteer Pub at 7 Priory Road which was a regular haunt of his as it was the nearest drinking establishment to his stable. Thomas Hinckley the landlord greeted him and knew him well as he usually came in on Tuesday market day. Frederick Charles Kisby, a long-term friend of Harold's was also in there. It was about 5.15pm and the pub was quite empty except for a children's party so he chatted to Harold and was surprised he only ordered a soda water before leaving. Fred had seen him in the cart about ten minutes earlier and had hailed him but got no response, probably because it was raining so hard.

Harold then returned to the stables and bedded down and fed the horse before walking home. He greeted his parents and washed up changing his dirty leggings before sitting down to tea. After the table was cleared he got out his accounts and aimlessly worked on them for a while. Then he put on his coat and headed for his local pub, the Foresters Arms which was just three hundred yards round the corner. He had arranged to meet up with his new girlfriend May Poole who worked in a drapery store and was the same age as him. This was to be his third date and he was looking forward to it. When he arrived at the pub at ten to seven she wasn't there but a good friend of his 18-year-old Frank Adams was at the bar. Frank was a family friend training to be a blacksmith with his father and lived a few doors down from Harold at 31 Woodside, next door to Harold's brother John at 33. They had a drink together and chatted until May arrived at quarter past seven, when Frank made a considerate departure to the bar. After having a good time Harold walked her home to Lodge Road and arrived home at 9.45pm going to bed soon after.

*

Meanwhile back at the O'Rourke household John and Frances were getting worried.

'Fran should be back by now shouldn't she?' Frances enquired.

'I'm sure she will be well on her way by now,' replied her husband unconvincingly.

'Well, you know I worry when she's out after dark.'

Her parents were expecting her to be back no later than five. It was now almost that time.

'Don't worry my dear she may have popped in to see her grandma or grandad at work.'

'Not in the winter though. She knows not to stop out after dark along that dangerous road. Those carters often don't have lamps on their wagons.'

Frances sat in the parlour cradling baby Bertha listening to the hall clock ticking the time away and getting increasingly worried of her daughter's whereabouts.

Five o'clock came and went, then five thirty and there was still no sign of her. By this time even John was pacing up and down and peering out the front window while his wife continued to become more agitated.

'Oh John, why didn't you give her bus fare to get back like you often do.'

'I know, don't you think I'm already blaming myself. I cannot bear to think that something might have happened to her. She's a sensible girl I'm sure all is well.'

By six o'clock they were both distraught and John had no other excuses to try and reassure his wife. Finally, Frances pleaded, 'It's been dark for an hour now John, where on earth can she be? You must do something.'

'I'll go and look for her. You stay here with the kids,' said John taking his coat from the hook, 'I may be a while as I'll walk into town to trace her route and hope to meet her coming back.'

'Please God, yes.'

He went out leaving his wife frantic and crying. He headed up the main road but didn't spot her. He was now breathless and panicky but began jogging all the way to Jenkinson's shop. Finding it closed he hurried to 6 Woodley Park Road where Phillip Bourdains lived, anxiously banging on the door which was opened by a rather startled Phillip.

'Oh, it's you John. Whatever's the matter?'

'It's Fran. She hasn't come home. Do you know anything?

14

'Sorry no. She left the shop before four with a parcel for you with more work. She didn't say she was going anywhere but home.'

Now in a traumatised state John spent the next hour visiting anywhere Fran might have stopped including her grandparents' house at 4 Garden Street in Tonbridge and the Baltic sawmills where her Grandad was employed but could not find any trace of her. He even went to the hospital in case she'd had an accident. He then rushed home hoping she had turned up in his absence to no avail. Hearing the news his wife almost collapsed and the other children were all crying. He informed her that he was going to report her missing to the police.

By this time, it was 8pm, so he hurried to the Southborough police station where they took details and said they would begin a search. They explained to him that they were on a different telephone system to the Tunbridge Wells Borough police station, and he should go to them and report her missing as well. It was one of the strange oddities of the time when the two police stations had no direct connection with each other. He hurried to Tunbridge Wells where they also took details and passed them on to officers on the beat who were advised to keep a look out for her and to check along the route.

John went back to the house to let his wife know the police were searching. She was prostrate with worry.

'I'll go out and carry on looking,' he told her.

'And I'm coming with you. I'll get next door to look after the kids.'

'Best you stay here love, in case she returns.'

'I'm coming with you and that's that,' she replied sternly.

The two of them were out until the early hours to no avail.

2.
New Year's Day 1902

Oh! what a scene of strife!
In her hair they found the knife,
'Tis said he violated her as well.
What a Wretch he must have been!
Dreadful was the scene.
What little Frances is suffered none can tell.

Thomas Doust and Joseph Nye, both farmhands, were walking to work along Vauxhall Lane, a journey they often made, idly chatting about the rough windy and wet night they endured and moaning about the chill wind that still persisted. The two-mile narrow byway was only used by workers needing to access the woods and hop fields situated behind stands and thickets of trees and brambles that lined the track. It was a very wild area climbing up steep brows and through deep cuttings where the banks had slipped exposing the roots of Ash and Hazel trees, their overhangs forming a roof over the track through which little light filtered. They were approaching the Vauxhall Inn, a popular hostelry at the top of the track at about 7.20am. The Inn had a small duck pond in front and a larger one to the side and rear some fifty yards away in a hollow. As they passed the larger pond, just before reaching the pub, they spotted what they believed to be a bundle of clothes dumped at the water's edge. They decided to investigate and approached the four feet high tarred wooden railing which was between the lane and the pond.

'What is that in the water, Joe?' asked Tom.

'Can't make it out, looks like a doll or something.'

'Too big for a doll. Looks like legs and boots sticking out of the water.'

They approached closer leaning on the fence that bordered the pond.

'Jesus, it's a body,' gasped Joe reeling back instinctively in horror.

'It looks like a girl.'

'Blimming hell, she's face down and that's her legs sticking out,' shouted Joe feeling sick. They were within seven feet of the body. Neither Tom or Joe were young men and had seen many sights in their lifetimes, but this shocked both of them. 'This is blooming awful, what are we going to do, Tom?'

'We need to check if she's alive?' he replied.

'No chance of that Tom. Look her head is under water. She must 'ave drowned.'

'But I can see blood on her,' Tom exclaimed.

'She must have been attacked or something. This ain't right. We need to inform the bobbies.' Joe seemed to be mesmerised by the sight of the boots sticking up out of the water and was just staring at them.

'Yeh, you're right. Come on Joe mate,' shouted Tom trying to shift Joe. 'We'd better get to the pub sharpish and rouse John Jefferey to raise the alarm.'

Both men hurried the fifty yards to the pub and banged loudly on the back door. 47-year-old John Jeffrey was the landlord and lived there with his wife Ellen and their two sons and daughter. They were finishing their breakfast when they heard the frantic banging and wondered what was up. John opened the door to find the two shocked men who babbled the news of their gruesome discovery. John and Ellen donned their coats and immediately hurried to the pond, where they too recoiled at the sight of the legs and lower part of the body protruding from the water. Ellen lingered back but John jumped over the fence and checked for any sign of life, but it was obvious the child had been dead for many hours.

17

John carefully pulled the body onto the bank and was sickened to see it was only partially clothed except for torn drawers, petticoat, black stockings and brown boots. He noticed a piece of red flannel chest protector on the bank and to his astonishment a partially opened clasp knife tangled in her hair. He could plainly see a gaping wound on her neck.

'This is no drowning. The poor girl has been killed,' he gravely informed the three onlookers, 'I'll send our lad for the constables. Don't touch anything or get close.'

He left the body on the bank still partially in the water. It was good half an hour before a police officer arrived. First on the scene was Constable William Horton of Southborough police. Like the others he was stunned at the sight before him, and it took a few seconds for him to react.

'I take it she is dead? he asked looking at John.'

'Yes I checked straight away. Been dead a while I'd say,' replied the landlord.

'I take it you never heard or saw anything last night.'

''fraid not. It was a stormy night, what with the wind and rain. Didn't hardly have a customer as no one wanted to traipse all the way out here, sad to say.'

The constable tentatively checked around and noticed the vague outline of wheel tracks next to the fence and the odd hoof print.

'I'd say they were made last night,' ventured the landlord over his shoulder.

'I think you're right John. I can't help looking at that ruddy knife in her hair. Damned peculiar if you ask me. Can't say I've ever seen such a thing.'

'You're right there. Something very strange about that.'

'Well, we better leave her be until my boss has seen it.'

Horton stood guard until Inspector James Savage; head of Southborough police arrived closely followed by other constables. Once the inspector had taken stock of the situation and had scanned the immediate area for evidence, his officers reverently removed the body to the stable block at the Inn. All of them were very upset by what they were seeing. It was common practice at the time to use inns and farm buildings to temporarily keep bodies that might require examination for a coroner's inquest. Realising the seriousness of the case and its implications Inspector Savage sent a message to his experienced superior, Robert James Styles the regional superintendent who was based at Tonbridge police station. He lived on the station premises with his wife and two teenage children, and he soon scrambled to the scene in a trap. The inspector also sent for Doctor Harry Manning Watts, the divisional police doctor for Tonbridge. Although mainly employed to look after the welfare of the men he was highly experienced having been a house surgeon at St Bart's hospital in London and they relied on his expertise in matters of assault and sexual offences.

Superintendent Styles was an old hand and had seen a lot of macabre scenes over his near thirty years' service, but again he was staggered by the awful situation presented to him. 'Have we established who the poor girl yet?'

'No, but we had a missing girl reported last night,' stated Inspector Savage, 'I'm guessing it has got to be her. Her parents were out all night searching for her along with us.'

'So, I've heard. She was only seven or eight years old?'

'That's right.'

'Has to be her then. How many young girls can there be missing at the moment. It would be too much of a coincidence if it's not but I'm no judge of kids ages,' said Styles.

'But you have a daughter don't you?' reminded Savage.

'I do. Edith. Not that young. She's fourteen and I can't imagine anything like this happening to her. It chills me to the bone,' said the obviously upset Styles. 'We had better get word to the parents to come and positively identify her as soon as possible before the word gets out. Perhaps you could do the honours so that it is dealt with as gently as possible. I know what I would be feeling like at this moment if it was my daughter. I cannot bear the thought of what they are going through with no word of her.'

'I'll get right on it. They would never have thought of looking up here for her.' The parents were given the terrible news at 9am and were both beyond consoling.

'The person responsible for this atrocity must have been a local in order to have known about this deserted place. Doesn't this area border the estate of Mr d'Avigdor Goldsmith, the Justice of the Peace?' Styles queried.

'Yes, he lives in the mansion yonder called Somerhill,' replied the Inspector.

'Might be worth asking there if they saw or heard anything, but I doubt it as its quite a distance. It'll be distressing for him to know that an innocent child was cruelly murdered within the hearing of his big mansion,' commented Styles.

Doctor Harry Watts, the divisional police surgeon was at home when he received the summons just after 9am and set off immediately arriving ten minutes later. He entered the barn to be greeted by the subdued police officers.

'Mornin' Harry. Terrible one this, I'm afraid,' said Styles greeting the doctor as he entered.

'So, I understand, Robert. What a thing to happen on New Year.'

'It looks like a nasty murder so I'd be grateful if you could give us some idea straight away of how and when she died. I have informed Thomas Buss the coroner.'

'I'll do my best but as you know I will have to do a post mortem to give you every detail.'

Before touching the body, the doctor gave Fran a visual inspection while Savage and Styles looked on.

'Well, obviously most of her clothing has been torn off which is not a good sign. Her pants look as though they were quite violently ripped. Have you found the rest of her clothing or where she was killed?'

'We have only just started looking, but no luck so far in the close vicinity,' answered Styles.

The doctor gently examined her private parts, and the officers turned their heads out of respect. 'I'm sickened to say she may have been raped, but there does not appear to be any defensive wounds,' he informed them.

'What kind of damned beast could have..,' exclaimed Savage lost for words.

'Oh, that's nasty as well,' said the doctor as he bent over Fran's body and closely scrutinised her neck, 'she has a deep long wound on the left side of her neck half way between the angle of her jaw and the anterior end of her collar bone.'

'So that's what obviously killed her do you think?'

'Well, it's very deep about an inch and a half and I would say severed her left carotid. If so she would have bled out very quickly.'

'How about time of death, Doc.'

'Well, I would say early yesterday evening, but don't take that as gospel for the time being.'

'So, we are looking for a murder scene with lots of blood?'

'Most definitely. Mm. Hello what have we got here? he exclaimed,' that's really odd. There's a half-opened clasp knife tangled up in her long thick hair. Never seen anything like that before.'

'Nor have any of us. The murder weapon do you think?'

'Too early to tell, I'm afraid, but I cannot see any other reason for it being there. Do you want me to remove it?'

'Not at the moment if you don't mind. I am calling in the detectives from Maidstone to take on the case and I would like them to see it in situ first,' explained Styles.

'As you wish. That's probably a good idea as this looks like a particularly brutal affair and will cause quite an outcry particularly as she may have been raped as well.'

The superintendent needed to track down the perpetrator quickly and realised that the case required the specialist services of the newly formed detective department based in the County town of Maidstone. Since its inception it was protocol to refer serious and complex cases to them which required "extra care and vigilance in following up or working out and collecting evidence" and this covered all twelve County police divisions.

A case involving the abduction, rape and murder of a young girl certainly fitted the criteria for their immediate involvement. He knew their department head Detective Sergeant Edwin Fowle quite well as he was the son of Thomas Fowle the superintendent of the Cranbrook division, a family friend and colleague. He arranged for a telegram to be sent post haste and awaited a reply.

To complicate matters he also had to liaise with the Tunbridge Wells Borough police, as the investigation was going to overlap into their jurisdiction. During this period each English County had a complicated mixture of County, town and borough police forces until they all amalgamated after the Second World War. Southborough was only a sub police station of the Tonbridge Division of the Kent County Constabulary which became the centre of operations having a lockup and courtroom attached. Styles knew that this was an horrendous and rare case which was bound to cause fear and anger in the local community and could possibly result in local civil disturbance. He also realised that it wouldn't

22

be long before they were deluged in press representatives from all over the County and London. He needed to keep a lid on everything for as long as possible.

He was soon proved right as news of the murder spread across the town and surrounding area like wildfire and when it was realised the victim was a child, the residents couldn't quite take in the horror of it all and that such a thing had occurred in their town. The local press and agents of the news agencies were soon all over the case and from mid-morning were tracking down the story. They related the news immediately with special editions, and the Press Association agent was soon on the case spreading the news nationwide. The *London Evening News* and *Manchester Evening News* were reporting the basic facts later that day. Such was the fever to sell newspapers that the vendors soon became a nuisance. The *Epsom Times* reported that a Charles Folgate, an excessively keen newspaper seller, travelled by train every day from London and stood outside Tonbridge Station constantly yelling at the top of his voice "Horrible murder at Tonbridge" So loud was he that complaints began to come in at the police station from residents and passengers alike. Police Constable Collins warned him several times without success and Charles was eventually fined nine shillings under a local byelaw which forbade "making a loud and continuous outcry by shouting."

The grisly details were gossiped over garden fences, on doorsteps, in shops and workplaces and like Chinese whispers became more and more disjointed from the actual facts. There was great anger which grew unabated and in intensity as the days passed. A correspondent of *The Daily News* described the atmosphere in their 3 January issue thus:

A feeling of terror seems to have taken possession of the district since the mysterious outrage on Monday last. Parents are afraid to let their little ones pass along unlighted roads after dark, and among the outlying cottages near Southborough I have met several young women who are not only afraid to go out but terrified of being left in the house alone." There was also a great and heartfelt expression of deepest sympathy for the parents of the unfortunate child. The local press increased the pressure on the police by reporting "It is hoped that in the course of a few hours, the perpetrator of one of the most heinous crimes would be found.

Once the superintendent had enough constables assembled he organised a search of the two-mile Vauxhall Lane while they awaited the detectives. He got the men to start from where the body was found and fan out specifically to try and discover where the murder and rape had taken place and hopefully recover the missing clothes. They had already searched round the pond for recent footprints or disturbance but found none other than those made by the pub landlord.

John and Frances O'Rourke were brought to the stable by cab with a police escort and arrived at 11am. John was supporting his wife as they entered the outbuilding to perform their harrowing task of identifying the body of their beloved daughter. The blanket that covered her was gently folded back to reveal her face. Both John and Frances stumbled backwards and had to be supported. It was evident to all present by their reaction that this was their daughter.

*

Police Illustrated News 11 January 1902

3.
Detective Fowle Takes Charge

Twenty-nine-year-old First-Class Detective Sergeant Edwin Fowle was standing in front of his mirror at his lodgings at 31 Melville Road in Maidstone adjusting his frock coat. He was five feet nine inches tall, broad shouldered and of stout stature with a well-groomed large moustache below a substantial nose. He was a religious man, had a somewhat questioning mind and a tenacious nature, perfect attributes for a detective. He was already getting a reputation for "always getting his man, or woman." He had joined the Kent police force ten years earlier on October 10, 1890, and moved into the dormitory barracks at their headquarters at Wrens Court in Maidstone for training before serving in several towns around the County of Kent over the next six years. He came from a police family; his father was a superintendent, his elder brother Thomas a sergeant and one of his uncles was in the police before becoming a railway detective. He was immediately acknowledged as a rising star with an aptitude for investigative work and was soon selected to join the newly formed detective department. He was in fact one of the first three detective constables on the force; a founding member of the department. His appointment brought him back full circle to Maidstone and being single he faced the prospect of having to reside in the austere barrack living quarters with forty other single constables which he did not fancy. So he had immediately sought lodgings.

He put the word out and luckily, a sergeant friend named John Kent heard of his plight and suggested inquiring with his elderly next door neighbour, 74-year-old widowed Annie Smith, who sometimes took in lodgers. She didn't hesitate in welcoming him as having a policeman in the house made her feel really secure, not that Edwin spent much time there being always on call and often leaving at all hours. What was somewhat disconcerting for him was that Annie had two spinster daughters Maria and Margaret living with her, who although ten years older than him gave him a lot of attention. But he did get mothered and looked after well and it was cheap.

It had recently become even more crowded when his younger 18-year-old brother Ivor decided to join the police as well. Edwin thought it better for him to bunk in with him until he got a posting, so Annie now had a feeling of double security and the police force had four Fowles in its ranks. More satisfying still for Edwin it also gave the three women someone younger to fuss over and took the attention off him. Edwin had been often chided by Annie that he should be courting and finding a wife for himself, an idea that Edwin didn't object to, but finding the time for such endeavours was difficult with his erratic lifestyle.

He took great care to dress smartly as he felt it gave him an air of authority and he liked to set a standard for his men. Being a plain clothes officer, he was given a clothes allowance of five pounds ten shillings a year, but he supplemented this in order to keep up his appearance; especially so as he had only been promoted a year before and appointed head of the Kent County Constabulary detective department. Although regulations insisted his jacket should have pockets that could accommodate a truncheon and handcuffs he ignored the need for a truncheon. He placed his still fashionable derby hat on his head and satisfied with his appearance he felt ready to face the morning. He had just managed to finish a substantial late fried breakfast cooked by Maria and although he had partaken in a little celebratory revelry the night before had managed to eat it and was suffering no ill effects. He never knew what the day would bring, but it was the uncertainty which excited him. His lodgings were only a few hundred

27

yards from the headquarters, so he always walked to work. Today though was to become one that he could have done without. At that moment there was a feverish knock on the front door, and he heard Maria open it and the sound of a familiar man's voice.

'You have a visitor,' Maria shouted up the stairs. Edwin descended and found Detective Constable George Fisher who was the same age as him and had become a detective at the same time as Edwin standing there. He had a telegram in his hand. They had a good working relationship and could recognise each other's moods. George was a good two inches taller than him, and Edwin sometimes found it disconcerting looking up at him, so he remained on the bottom step of the staircase.

'Urgent one for you sergeant, just in,' said George formally, 'and a bad one if you don't mind me saying.'

Edwin read the note and his face soon turned to a grimace, while George who knew what the message was about stood with a tight face.

'It's not going to be a happy new year, eh George?' he said, 'Well, come on then, we better get there straight away, and I'll obviously need you with me. I believe this is going to be a testing investigation and your local knowledge may come in handy.' Edwin knew George hailed from the village of Speldhurst, on the outskirts Tunbridge Wells not far from the murder scene. 'Any idea when the next train is to Tonbridge?'

'No idea.'

'Get back to headquarters George and find Henry for me and tell him he is on the case as well. That will please him. It will be good experience for him,' Edwin told George. 26-year-old Henry Petley was the second of the three detective constables on Edwin's small team and had a year less on the force than George who liked to act as his senior. The third experienced detective, 30-year-old Alfred

28

Wratten, was to remain at base to pick up any other urgent investigations.

'Henry is already waiting expectantly for your orders,' smiled George.

'Oh and get someone to send a telegram to Superintendent Styles to say we are on our way. I'll meet you at the station.' The electric telegraph was the only form of relatively quick communication apart from sending a message by road. George went rushing off back to tWrens Cross police station. Edwin collected a few bits and pieces and put them in a bag as he had a feeling he would not be back that night. He opened the front door, turned, and shouted, 'Maria, I probably won't be back tonight.' Maria who was sitting in the kitchen drinking tea with her mother Annie, didn't respond but just turned to her and raised her eyebrows.

'A murdered seven-year-old. What a start to the new year,' he muttered to himself as he headed for the station.

*

Edwin was fascinated by trains and enjoyed any chance to ride the rails. He had continued an almost childish fascination with them. He viewed them almost as living entities with their noise and smell, the hissing steam, their intricate moving parts topped off with their screaming whistles. He watched out the window as the smoke from the accelerating train flew past and could see the early morning frost gradually retreating under the leaden sky which only added to his solemn mood. The three men sat in silence for a while and George, sitting opposite with Henry, was watching Edwin's face. He knew his boss was in one of his contemplative moods probably deliberating how he was going to manage this challenging murder which might turn out to be the most high profile one he had dealt with since becoming chief. George nudged Henry and nodded towards Edwin indicating to him to start a conversation.

'This case we're going on is going to be a big one don't you think,' ventured Henry.

'Indeed, it will be. One of those cases which I bet will unfortunately remain in your memory for the whole of your careers. Mind you, if we manage to catch the beggar it will be a boost for all our careers,' said Edwin and turned to look out the window again returning to his thoughts. He was relishing the opportunity, but the responsibility was weighing heavy on his mind. He remained silent throughout the rest of the journey while George and Henry chatted excitedly.

When they arrived at Tonbridge station they were met by a local uniformed constable driving a trap. Only the officers with the rank of superintendent or above had their own horse drawn two wheeled cart or trap and Superintendent Styles had sent his to collect them. They were also used to transport prisoners to the Maidstone and Canterbury gaols. It was going to be a cramped and uncomfortable journey as the trap was not designed for four occupants. Edwin sat with the constable at the front while the other two squashed into the rear.

'It's a terrible thing that's happened sir,' he stated.

'We can all agree on that constable,' replied Edwin.

'The superintendent has asked me to take you up to the body immediately and he will meet you there.'

'That's fine with us. The sooner we get started the better.'

'There is a big crowd at the police station already. I ain't seen anything like it before.'

'I'm sure you haven't. In cases like this people start to panic and rumours abound,' said Edwin climbing into the carriage.

An irate, worried and upset crowd had indeed gathered outside both Southborough and Tonbridge police stations in fear of the safety of their own children and demanding news of the murder. Officers were having to be deployed to prevent any trouble.

'I'm going to take you on a back street to avoid passing the police station and straight up to the pub where the body is,' announced the constable. Ten minutes later the officers were climbing down at the Vauxhall Inn where Superintendent Robert Styles was standing by the duck pond at the front to greet them.

'Hello, Edwin how are you. Sorry to land this on you as I know how busy you are, but it is a rum business and I need all the help I can get.'

'Hello Robert, not at all. This is the kind of case we were established for,' replied Edwin. He knew the superintendent from other cases and had in fact just recently been working on a matrimonial fraud case in Tonbridge with him. Both men were well aware that now he had called in Edwin, he would be nominally in charge of the investigation and the one who would shoulder any criticism that might accrue. Ultimately the unit was autonomous and only reportable to the Chief Constable, but under operational orders in these situations Edwin had to supply a daily report of progress to the superintendent in charge of whichever division he was operating in. Armed with the evidence discovered by the detectives, the superintendent was responsible for working up the case for any possible arrest, charge and trial.

The officers went into the stable and the blanket was drawn back to reveal the body which was described "as having one hand clenched and the other lying on her chest while her face was set in angelic calmness." There was complete silence for a while as Edwin took in the scene.

'I know we see some terrible sights nearly every week Robert but to me it is incomprehensible that anyone could do such a thing.'

'I know what you mean, Edwin,' the superintendent replied gravely. 'I have had a word with Thomas Buss the County coroner, and he has agreed to delay the opening of the inquest until 4.30pm on Friday to give us a chance to put together the circumstances of the case. He could not delay it any longer because of his legal obligations.'

'No, that sounds fine. Good of him.'

The superintendent then explained to Edwin what the doctor's initial assessment was regarding cause and time of death.

'I agree that its damn strange about the knife. If it is the murder weapon why on earth would you leave it in the girl's hair. Why not dispose of it? Most odd.'

They then walked over to the murder scene and the position of the body was pointed out to him.

'Whoever killed her must have known this spot well and was aware how isolated it is. He knew he could easily dispose of the body unobserved in the darkness. Also, the pond is in a hollow and probably not overlooked by the Inn.'

'We have been all round the pond and haven't found any footprints or drag marks in the wet mud but have discovered recent hoof marks and wheel ruts here. We reckon it was a small four-wheel cart rather than a larger waggon with two horses. Last night's rain has obliterated some of the marks,' the superintendent informed Edwin pointing.

'Oh yes, I see,' commented Edwin as he crouched and looked at the tracks from different angles, 'looks as though the cart was backed up to within two feet of the fence.'

'Our hypothesis so far is that whoever did it threw the body from the back of the cart without getting down off it.'

'Could be, but it's a bit of a distance, six feet at least wouldn't you say. She is quite a big girl from what I could see?'

'The girl weighs about seventy pounds give or take, so I think we are probably looking for someone quite big and strong.'

'Or someone just strong; used to lifting and carrying.

'How is the search of the lane going?'

'I have got as many as I can spare on it, but as you see we are already getting morbid onlookers turning up and I'm having to put officers on guard here.'

'It's most annoying,' agreed Edwin, 'I don't know what they expect to see. With your permission Robert I'll get my men to begin inquiries in Southborough, and I will go and see the parents. I'm not looking forward to it, I can tell you.'

*

Meanwhile Police Corporal Charles Castle of Southborough police was supervising the search along the two-mile-long Vauxhall Lane. They had spent all morning doing a cursory examination of the verges along its length but had no luck in finding any discarded clothes, pools of blood or any signs of where the murder may have taken place. In the afternoon they began a more intensive check in the areas behind the hedgerows and in the woods and fields. He was cursing all the sightseers that were hampering his men and trying to move them on. At about 1.45pm Charles was about three hundred and fifty yards along the lane from the Southborough end, not far from Manor Farm, when he looked over a gate and behind a six-foot-high hedge into a small wood. He immediately spotted a white straw hat with black band hanging from the bramble bushes. He climbed over the gate and as he neared the hat discovered more clothing scattered in a radius of six feet in the bushes. It appeared the items had been thrown over the hedge. He carefully disentangled a blue serge frock, a pink flannelette petticoat, a chemise which was torn from top to bottom, a white linen scarf and a large man's white handkerchief. All the garments were soaked from the rain.

As he was about to climb back over the gate he spotted more clothing about twelve feet further along. His heart was pounding with the adrenaline of the find. He shouted to a colleague to hold onto the clothes he had already retrieved and went to investigate. He found an ulster cape hanging from another bush, so he grabbed that as well. He noticed stains on the bottom of the petticoat which might be blood and most of the clothes were torn. He realised the importance of the finds and sent a runner to inform the superintendent and quickly made his way to the police station with them. His discovery was over a mile and a half from the body. On the way back he chastised himself for missing them that morning.

Meanwhile Edwin, had introduced himself to John and Frances at their home and completed a difficult and emotional interview with them. He was at Tonbridge police station by mid-afternoon and arrived just as Corporal Castle appeared with the clothing. Castle spotted Edwin and rushed up to him beaming.

'Look what I have found sergeant,' he excitedly said thrusting a bundle at Edwin.

'What have you got here?' inquired Edwin taking them.

'A girl's clothes thrown over the hedge in Vauxhall Lane. They must be hers.'

'Well done Castle. If they are you may have found the murder scene.'

'Got to be as there is blood on them.'

'Go back and make sure the area is sealed off will you. I'll be along later after I have examined these finds,' he ordered the constable, 'This could be our first breakthrough if we have found the murder scene,' he muttered to himself as he watched the constable hurry away. Once Edwin had studied the clothes and made notes he was taken to

Vauxhall Lane and was soon aware how desolate it was, with no visible habitation and just a narrow track between overhanging trees interspersed with the occasional field. He could imagine how grim it would be at night. He was shown the spot of the discoveries by Castle and inquired, 'any sign of where the murder took place?'

'I'm afraid not, sir. The problem is it rained heavy last night with a hefty wind and could have washed away any lying blood on the grass.'

'Quite so, but according to the Doc there would have been pints of the stuff, as it would have spurted out like a fountain for a couple of feet, and you'd think some was still visible.'

'Well, we will keep searching but I don't hold out much hope. He may have killed her elsewhere and just dumped the clothes here on his way out.'

Edwin wandered up the lane for a while deep in thought and then returned to the police station.

*

The Vauxhall Inn around the period

Va

uxhall Lane. Still a foreboding place after dark today.
[Author photo]

4.
A Possible Suspect

Detectives George Fisher and Henry Petley were already in the town tracking down witnesses. In Southborough, Tonbridge and Tunbridge Wells the news of the murder and the finding of the body was spreading quickly and continually being updated. Being a small community, it did not take long for residents to discover the identity of the victim and the circumstances. Everyone was shocked into disbelief that such a vile incident could occur in their peaceful village. Luckily for the police there were many people heading home from work and shopping along the main thoroughfare of St John's Road as the light faded. Witnesses began to come forward who had seen Fran that afternoon.

One was a Julia Hollamby who was staying with her sister-in law in Powder Mill Lane not far from the Cross Keys public house on the corner of St John's road. She told George that she was walking side by side with her sister-in-law when she pointed out a horse and cart being driven by a young man at excessive speed. She noticed the horse was sweating and also that there was a young girl sitting in the front wearing a white straw hat and brown jacket.

'What time was this?' asked George.

'It was about 4.30pm.'

Several youngsters who lived near Fran also believed they had spotted her. One was 13-year-old Rose Emily Dupont who lived in Edward Street adjoining the street where Frances lived. She too was walking home along the St John's Road to Southborough and actually overtook her and made a passing comment asking what was in the parcel she was carrying. Rose glanced round further on and saw her sitting in a dark coloured cart pulled by a brown horse with a young man in dark clothes driving it.

'Did you see her get onto the cart?' asked Henry.

'No, I didn't, but she must have crossed the road to get in.'

'Did the girl look upset?'

'Not that I could see.'

14-year-old Ethel Agnes Muggeridge who also lived round the corner from Fran in Forge Road and had seen her walking towards her home about half a mile before Cross Keys sometime between 4.30pm to 4.45pm just as it was getting dark. She saw her crossing the road and climbing up into a four wheeled dark coloured cart drawn by a large brown horse. She spotted a black parcel in her hand, and she was wearing a white hat. She slipped a couple of times as she wasn't tall enough the reach the step.'

'Who was driving it?' asked Henry.

'A young man in dark clothes wearing a hat.'

'Did you recognise him?'

'No. sir.'

'Then what happened?'

'The man slapped the reins, and the horse took off quite quickly down the road.'

'Which way did it go?'

'Towards Southborough where Frances and I live.'

They received another important breakthrough when Constable Kent struck lucky when a 77-year-old cab driver from Vale Road Tonbridge named Conrad Smith approached him. He had heard about the murdered girl, and he believed he had seen a young girl in a cart in the area at the time of the abduction.

'I was driving down the hill past the Cross Keys pub in my cart from the High Brooms direction at about 4.30 to 4.45pm, I can't be sure exactly. I don't have a watch you see.'

'And you saw a child in this cart.'

'That's right, sitting next to the driver.'

'Why do you remember.'

'Well, you see the cart belongs to the Apted's; you know the old coal merchant.'

'So, you recognised the driver?'

'Of course. It was his son Harold. Him and his cart are well known round here.'

'You know him well do you?

'Not well, but I've spoken to him many times.'

'And it was definitely him?'

'It was getting dark, and he didn't have a light on the cart, so I couldn't see him well, but yes it was him alright.'

'And he had a child with him.' Kent persisted.

'Well, as I said it was getting dark, but there was something by his side. Looked like a child.'

'So, you are not actually sure?'

'Pretty sure.'

Conrad was to become a key witness but unfortunately for the police he later rescinded part of his statement and asked that the section about seeing the girl was over written to say that he was not definite.

Then Henry spoke to a William Earnest Cox, a scaffolder who lived in Ford Street and had come forward with information. He and his workmates had been working in Vauxhall Lane that day and were heading home as dusk fell.

'What did you see Mr Cox?'

'Well, me and my six mates had knocked off work and were all coming down the lane, some of us pushing the handcart which had some leftover wood on it.'

'And what time was this?'

'Must have been about five thirty, I'd say.'

'And?' encouraged Henry.

'I saw a light in the road about three hundred yards yonder and as we got closer saw it was a cart light. It was stationary, and we slowed up a bit and started listening in case we could hear anything. Not often you see anyone using the lane at that time of evening, so we thought 'allo, bet 'es got a woman with him. You know what I mean. As we got close the cart moved off and came towards us and we laughed thinking we had ruined his evening.'

'Did you see who was in it.'

'Can't say I did. It was pretty dark, and the cart light was low.'

'No idea at all. You must have been close?' persisted the detective.

'Nah, sorry. It went past quite quick, but I know the cart.'

You do!,' Henry almost shouted.

'I've seen the cart often at the market on a Tuesday. It has lades down the side and back to keep the animals in. Not many like that.'

Henry asked excitedly, 'Do you know who owns it?'

'No, I don't but you could ask some of the other lads who were with me, or I reckon anyone at the market could probably tell you.'

'Can you give me their names?'

'Sure.'

Both Constable Kent and Henry relayed their exciting news to Edwin and the superintendent. Edwin said to Henry, 'get the boys onto it now and find these other workers. I think we're on to something.'

He then turned to the superintendent, 'that cart was sighted parked only a few yards from where the discarded clothes were and heading up towards the Vauxhall Inn and fits the time frame as far as we understand it. It is too much of a coincidence. It has got to be our man.'

'Looks that way,' agreed Styles.

The workmates of William were soon found and interviewed. Arthur Henry Bridgeland was one of them and said he hadn't seen the light as he was looking down as he pulled the cart. 'I thought I saw a girls legs walking the other side of the cart by the hedge as it passed us.'

'It was definitely a girl you say. Did you see her?'

'Nah, she kept pace with the cart. Only saw the bottom of her dress, not her head or anything else.'

Frederick Jenner was another of the workmen, 'I can't say for certain that I saw any girl, but I thought I did. We had been laughing together as we approached the cart thinking that the driver probably had a woman with him. You know what I mean,' he winked. 'We stopped for a rest, hoping to listen. You know how it is, when us lads get together. I thought I had seen someone on the other side of the cart and saw something dark between the wheels but couldn't swear to it. It might have been a shadow.'

It had been a long day for the detectives and was now early evening. When Edwin was told about the statements he was somewhat disappointed as there was no firm sighting of Fran, but she could of course have been lying dead in the back of the cart when it passed the men in the lane. He went in search of the superintendent to ask his advice on whether there was enough evidence to warrant a visit to this young man mentioned by Conrad Smith.

'It's obvious from all the witness interviews so far that we are looking for a young carter with a four wheeled cart and a dark coloured horse who knows the area well and therefore must be local. Some of the witnesses confirm that the cart could belong to a Mr Apted and driven by his son,' Edwin informed Styles.

'From what you have told me I totally agree, but so far we only have the word of two young school girls, an old man with suspect eyesight who believes it might be Harold Apted and a group of men who have little conclusive information except the one who reckons he recognises the cart. None of them actually place this Apted fellow in Vauxhall Lane at the time.'

'But he did mention the distinctive boarding down the side of the cart and was pretty adamant,' persevered Edwin.

'Can you imagine how many similar carts there are in the town and who knows how many may have boarding for carrying livestock.'

'Do we know anything about the Apted family?' queried Edwin.

'Yes. Old Tom Apted has been a well-known coal merchant in the town for decades and raised a family of eleven children, none of whom to my knowledge have been in trouble. Harold is the youngest and still lives at home and now does most of the work as old Tom isn't up to it anymore.'

'We need to have a chat with the market traders as well to see what we can discover about Apted.'

'But I reckon this Harold Apted is the most promising lead we have and must be worth a visit.'

'Indeed, I agree and the sooner the better so that no possible evidence goes astray. We might as well get to it now and I will come with you.'

'It's a filthy evening out there,' stated Edwin peering out the window.

'I know. What a dreary beginning to the new year.'

*

It was raining heavily when Edwin and Styles went to 69 Woodside Road, the home of the Apted family. It was 8pm when they knocked on the door. Edwin was in plain clothes and Styles in his uniform. It was answered by an elderly man.

'Good evening sir. Sorry to disturb you so late but I am Detective Sergeant Fowle of Kent County Constabulary, and this is Superintendent Styles who you may recognise, and we are here on an urgent and serious matter. May I ask your name?.

'My name is Thomas Apted, but what on earth do you want?' he responded.

'We would like a word with your son Harold if we may.'

'Whatever for?' challenged the father.

'We would prefer to speak to him first.'

'Well, e's not here.'

'Will he be back soon?

'We are a respectable family sergeant, and not used to police visits late at night. What's it all about?' said Thomas irritably.

Edwin asked again. 'Please Mr Apted when do you expect him back?'

'He normally gets in from the pub about ten o'clock. He has to get up early for work.'

Edwin said, 'Well then sir we will have to return then.'

'I'd rather you didn't. Can't this wait until the morning?'

'I'm afraid not,' interjected the superintendent.

The two officers ran back to their waiting cab to get out of the rain and headed back towards Tonbridge police station. Styles asked, 'Do you reckon he was there?'

'Hard to tell. His father could be covering for him, but we'll see what happens at ten o'clock.'

'What a horrible night. I suggest we go to my rooms rather than wait in the station. I think a nice brew is in order, don't you?'

Edwin agreed and a few minutes later thay were sitting in front of the fire in the superintendents quarters drying out while sipping their tea.

'I was so sorry to hear about your mother, Edwin. Such a tragedy being so young. How is your old man holding up?'

Edwin's mother Margaret had died a few months earlier following an unsuccessful operation in a London hospital and had suffered a painful death. Edwin had been devoted to her and was still coming to terms with it, so rarely wanted to talk about it. Styles was a friend of the family knowing Edwin's father Thomas well. His superintendent father was one of the longest serving officers on the Force. The couple were so loved and well respected that Margaret had been given a police funeral with six constables as pall bearers and an Inspector, three sergeants and twenty constables marching in the cortege.

'You know my father; he avoids his grief by spending most of his time keeping busy working all hours.'

'I can understand that. How about you?'

'I'm getting used to her not being around and as brothers we have all consoled each other, but Ivo being the youngest has taken it the worst.'

'Of course. It is not good to lose a mother when you're an eighteen-year-old.'

The two men lapsed into silence and Edwin sat drumming his fingers on the arms of the chair. Both men were clock watching and eager to interview Harold Apted. It was still raining when the two got back into the waiting carriage which rattled down the deserted streets, the horse's hooves echoing in the quietness. They reached the house just after 10pm. This time the father allowed them in without argument. His wife Ellen was standing in the hall with him looking scared.

'Good evening Mrs Apted. Sorry to drip water all over your hallway. Has your son returned home now?'asked Edwin.

'He's upstairs in bed asleep.'

'Is he. I thought he might have waited up for us.'

'I'll call him.'

'Don't bother we can go up and find him. Excuse me,' and they pushed past the couple.

At that moment a young man dressed in his trousers and an open shirt appeared at the top of the stairs. As he descended Edwin noticed he was of a short stature and looked younger than his age.

'What's happening father?'

'It's the police from earlier son wanting a word. Whatever it is you don't have to speak to them.'

Edwin called up. 'Harold Apted?'

'Yes.'

'We need to have a word with you about a serious incident that occurred last night.'

'Really, why?'

'You may be able to help us with our inquiries. Can you account for your whereabouts yesterday afternoon and evening, say from 4pm to 10pm.'.

'You don't have to answer that son.'

'I don't mind father; I have done nothing wrong.' Harold said calmly.

'You don't seem that worried about our visit late at night.'

'As I said I have done nothing wrong, and I am pleased to help if I can.'

'So where were you last evening,' Styles asked.

Harold explained that he was working and had travelled all over town and was finally asked:

'Which way did you come home last night?'

'I came down the Camden Road, through High Brooms and along Powder Mill Lane, then through Southborough and down Quarry Hill and home.'

'Did you go out again?'

'I did drive out the stable again to deliver a coal bill to Mrs Scott. She lives at the top house on the left-hand side of Primrose Hill.'

45

Styles who obviously knew the area well asked 'Is that your usual route home from High Brooms; bit of a long way round wouldn't you say?'

Apted replied, 'I had to call on Mr Semple at his slaughterhouse for my Christmas box.'

'Did you see anyone that can verify that' asked the superintendent.

'I saw no one. Neither did I at the top house at Primrose Hill.'

What time did you get back to your yard?'

'I got back about 5.30pm.'

Edwin asked, 'Where is the clothing you were wearing yesterday?'

'Why on earth are you asking about his clothes?' interjected the father angrily.

Again, Edwin ignored the question.

Harold answered, 'Upstairs in my bedroom.'

'We need to examine them,' said Styles.

'Whatever for,' blustered his exasperated father.

Harold grabbed a candle off the table and Edwin followed him closely up the steep staircase in the gloom to his bedroom. The room had the stale fetid smell of animals and unwashed humans making Edwin wince. He watched Harold remove a dark blue jacket from a hook behind the door. It was quite dark in the bedroom with just the one candle lighting it, so Edwin took the candle off Harold and held it near the jacket to examine it and he noticed something on the left shoulder. It was difficult to make out in the shadow, but it looked like blood to him. Quite a thick smear of congealed blood in two stripes.

Edwin asked, 'These look like blood stains to me. How did they get there?'

Apted replied, 'I'm in and out of slaughterhouses all the time and often get blood on me. I expect the stain is from when I went into Mr Semple's place.'

'Where are the rest of your clothes?'

'Downstairs in the front room.'

They went back down, and Apted picked up a pair of drab coloured brown knee britches, brown leggings, a dark check cap and a pair of boots and placed them on a chair. 'That's all of them unless you want my underwear?' he cheekily added.

Edwin ignored him and sifted through the garments on the chair taking a cursory look at them and then inquired, 'Do you own a knife?'

Apted replied, 'A knife. No. I've never owned one in my life.'

'Really. That seems very strange in your line of work.'

'No never,' he repeated.

'Put a coat on as you will have to accompany us to the police station. We will keep hold of these.' Edwin indicated the clothes as he picked them up.

'You are joking,' exclaimed the father.

'I'm afraid not,' said Styles.

'But whatever for?'

'Because we are investigating a serious crime and have found blood on your son's clothing.'

'But he has just explained where it might be from. It can be a messy job. Is this to do with the murder of the child?' his father hesitantly inquired.

'You have heard about it then?'

'Well of course it is all over town. You cannot seriously think that my boy has anything to do with it. He's a respectable lad,'

'We are just making inquiries of people who were seen in the vicinity.'

'Who says he was there?'

'It's alright father I know nothing about it.'

'I believe you own a horse and cart?'

47

'Of course, he does, we are a coal merchant and make deliveries.' interrupted his irritated father.

Edwin was getting annoyed with the father's outbursts and said to Harold, 'We need to examine your cart Mr Apted. Could we do it now. Where is it?'

'This is outrageous,' stated the frustrated father, 'it's down the road in my yard.'

'Will you please show us where it is, Harold?'

Harold declared, 'It's dark down there and you won't see anything. Why not come back in the morning.'

'I'm sorry it has to be done now.'

The three men left the house, and the rain was still coming down in torrents. It was just over half a mile to the yard at the corner of Priory Street and Pembury Road. It was very dark, but they had a couple of lanterns which gave a subdued light. The officers stood with water dripping from their hat brims and capes while Harold unlocked the chained gate, and they entered the stable yard. Parked there was a four-wheel cart, which they examined by the light of the lanterns. It appeared to be of a chocolate colour. Edwin peered into the back of the cart where there was some straw covering the wooden planked floor.

'Let's check the stable,' Edwin said to Styles, and he opened the barn door. Inside was a dark brown and very old looking horse which let out a quiet whimper at the intrusion although in the poor light of the lantern it was difficult to confirm the horses actual colouring. Edwin and Styles then gave the interior a cursory search. On the left as they stepped in was a shelf and Edwin spotted something lying there.

Edwin exclaimed, 'what have we got here then,' and held up a very wet man's white pocket handkerchief. Edwin examined it closely and turned to Apted and said, 'This looks as though it has been recently washed, is it yours?'

Apted replied, ' I use it to groom my horse with, so what.'

Edwin smelt the handkerchief and there was no odour of a horse.'

'Are you sure about that?'

I told you; I washed it.'

'Strange thing to use on a horse though isn't it?' asked Edwin as he handed the item to the Styles. 'We will be taking this back to the station.'

It was impossible to thoroughly search the building with lanterns so Edwin decided that it would be better to come back in daylight. He then turned to Apted and said, 'You will now have to come with us to Tonbridge police station for further questioning and I will be taking your jacket and handkerchief to a doctor to be forensically examined. Do you understand?'

Apted just replied, 'Am I under arrest?'

'Not at the moment, you are just helping us with our inquiries.'

'Alright, then,' said Apted sullenly.

The two officers escorted him back to Tonbridge police station where Edwin examined all the items in the better light. He didn't make Apted remove his shirt but checked him over and discovered a blood stain on the outside of the left sleeve that corresponded with the stain on the jacket.

'Do you understand why you have been brought to the station?'

Apted nonchalantly replied, 'Oh yes, I suppose it is something to do with the little girl in Vauxhall Lane. I was sure that's what you were inquiring about when you asked about the blood.'

'So, I don't have to spell it out.'

'No.'

Edwin then detained Apted in a cell at the station while he took the suspect's jacket and the handkerchief to the surgery of Dr Watts who examined them while Edwin looked on.

Edwin asked, 'Any initial comments, doctor?'

Dr Watts answered, 'Well it appears the stain on the left sleeve of the jacket is blood, animal or human who knows, and it has soaked through the lining so it must have been quite copious. I will have to do tests of course to be sure it is blood.'

'Thank you doctor. Sorry to disturb you so late in the evening.'

'Not a problem. Doctor's are used to such intrusions.'

Edwin returned to the station and got Constable Earnest Tugwell the lock up keeper, to release Apted from the cell, and said to him, 'We will be investigating further and will probably need to speak to you again. In the meantime, you can go home. We are keeping your items for further examination.'

'If you have to.'

Harold's concerned older brother Charlie had been informed of events by his father and had hurried to the police station to discover what was happening and to give his brother support. The two of them left the station and went home. It was now midnight and too late for Edwin to go back to Maidstone, so he stayed the night with Styles and his family. They stayed up into the early hours discussing the case over a nightcap.

'This girl's father must take some responsibility for her death,' Edwin said suddenly.

'That seems somewhat unfair. Why do you say that?' replied Styles somewhat surprised by Edwin's statement.

'Well as you know I'm not a father, but I cannot believe it right to send a girl that age to walk a five-mile return journey at twenty past two carrying packages on a winters afternoon when its dark by four thirty,' Edwin explained.

'It's not ideal, I admit, but it's the age we live in Edwin. Kids are expected to work long hours and be out late from an early age, but I am surprised he left it so late to send her. I know I wouldn't be happy sending my daughter out so near to dark.'

'I didn't take a liking to that lad Apted. Seemed too cocky to me.'

'I must admit he did seem particularly unconcerned about our visit.'

'I have a feeling we have found our man.'

Styles smiled. 'The old policeman's nose, eh Edwin?'

'Something like that, but we have got to prove it.'

*

Thursday was going to be a busy day in the investigation which the two officers hoped would result in an arrest. Edwin intended to hold a briefing first thing for his troops and later there was to be a post mortem of the body and they also had an upsetting and stressful task to perform which neither man was looking forward to; the identification by her parents of the clothing found discarded in Vauxhall Lane.

On Thursday morning Edwin held the briefing with his detectives and various uniformed officers from the two local constabularies who had been seconded to help in the investigations. They all sat or lounged against the walls in an excited mood as they had all heard about their senior officers visit to the Apted house and yard the previous evening. There had been much station gossip about it. Edwin, the superintendent and Inspector Savage entered the room to a hush.

'We now have a prime suspect gentlemen and we need to find out all about our Mr Harold Apted,' announced Edwin. 'Track down his friends and workmates, anyone he has done work for. Check his normal routine. Listen to all the local gossip about him that is doing the rounds. We need to discover who the real Harold Apted is, not the choir boy image he professes to be. Priority is to try and find out about the knife found in her hair. Did Harold own one and specifically this one. Interview anyone you can find connected with the market, anyone who had seen his movements at his yard and stables on the day of the murder and following day. Time is against us if we are to arrest him. We need tangible witnesses and evidence.

Henry, George and the uniformed constables set off with some excitement at the task ahead and were dispatched across Southborough, Tunbridge Wells and Tonbridge making house to house inquiries, chatting to people in the main streets and interviewing witnesses who had come forward.

Soon after the briefing John and Frances O'Rourke arrived at the station to be met by Edwin who took them to inspect all the clothing. The items had been laid out on a table and on entering the room both parents immediately gasped at the sight of them and staggered into the room, their grief plain on their haunted faces.

Edwin quietly said, 'I am sorry to put you through this, but can you confirm that these are the clothes that Fran was wearing when she disappeared?'

John supported his wife by the arm and they both nodded unable to speak but then Frances exclaimed, 'the white handkerchief. It is not hers!'

'Are you sure?'

'Yes. That is not hers. Don't tell me that belongs to the murderer,' she shrieked.

'That remains to be seen,' reflected Edwin.

Edwin watched sorrowfully as the two shambled out of the room accompanied by a constable to be taken home.

*

While they had been viewing the clothing Dr. Harry Watts was examining Fran's body again this time with another local specialist doctor named Edward Stewart Cardell. This was at the request of the Coroner. They reported later that her organs were quite healthy and there was food in the stomach probably consumed three to four hours before her death as it was nearly digested and there was no doubt the child had been "outraged." There was a bruise just below the right collar bone probably caused at the same time as the stabbing. There was a wound half way down the left side of the neck, half an inch wide and one and a half inches deep penetrating the muscles and the carotid artery. It would have caused a great deal of bleeding spurting out like a fountain and spreading a couple of feet from the body and she would have bled out in about ninety seconds.

The two concluded that considerable force must have been used and from the angle would be by a right hand. They confirmed the wound could have been caused by the knife found entangled in her hair and estimated the time of death to be twelve hours before recovery of the body. Fran was dead before being put in the pond and there were no signs of a struggle.

When Edwin read their report he realised that somewhere there must be a murder scene with a large obvious pool of blood, and he needed to find it. He did not think that the findings greatly helped his case as Apted only had small amounts of blood on his clothing and there was no evidence so far that he had changed clothes. The lack of blood on the pocket knife also worried him.

During the course of Thursday, the police team had scoured the community for witnesses and dozens of residents were interviewed, many of which came forwards of their own accord. The community was keen to help in any way they could and luckily for the police there had been many residents around at the time of the murder. They collected dozens of statements of sightings and the movements of Harold Apted.

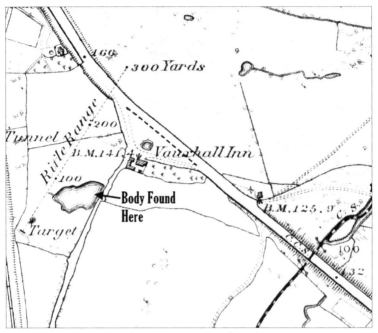

Where Frances was found.

*Cart similar to the one owned by the Apteds but had been
modified with wooden planked sides.*

5
Detective Fowle Investigates

A home once so bright filled with gloom and despair.
There's one we have missed, we cannot find her there,
She who we loved and cherished thro' life,
Why kill her and cause all this sad grief and strife,
Poor little Frances. why take her away?
What harm had she done then, why should they say?

Friday 3 January was to prove a hectic and tiring day for all those involved but there was to be no let up. Edwin was at the police station soon after dawn collating all the statements his men had taken the previous day and sorting out the most relevant and telling. By lunchtime these amounted to a possible twenty people being subpoenaed to court. He felt he had a compelling case for suspecting Apted for the murder, but it was only his job to gather the evidence and present it to the superintendent for evaluation; it was up to him to sanction any action. He was keen to get a warrant that day to arrest Apted, but he needed a pretty watertight case to present to the superintendent and magistrate. He knew he couldn't afford to get it wrong not with all the pressure from the press. Although doubts had been raised about Apted's ability to throw a body from a cart into the pond he had re-enacted the scenario with George and Henry and they had come to the conclusion that it was a "hell of a throw," but possible. Edwin was relatively happy with all the statements George, Henry and other officers had obtained, but many of them seemed to contradict Apted's movements on New Year's Eve.

A lady named Sarah Hollamby, who lived on Powder Mill Lane, was familiar with Apted and his cart regularly passing her house from the market laden with calves. She saw it pass by between one and two that afternoon and later about 4.40pm she was walking with her visiting sister-in-law Julia along St Johns Road. Both ladies noticed the same cart approaching from Tunbridge Wells. It caught Sarah's attention as the driver was standing up and she said to Julia, 'That horse has had a good doing, see how it is sweating' Julia had said nothing at the time but next morning insisted she had seen a child sitting in the back, not on the seat but as though she was sitting on something. She told Henry that the girl "was wearing a light hat with a black band, and something light round the shoulders.'

Edwin was puzzled by the fact that Sarah had not seen the child and that Julia had not mentioned it to her. The fact that she had added such detail later made him wonder if she had read the facts in a newspaper or heard talk. Henry had told him she couldn't read or write so it was doubtful, but Edwin had pointed out she was not deaf so may have overheard something. Still it was very compelling testimony and did place Fran in the cart. A photographer named Thomas Dean had also been interviewed who insisted he knew Harold well and definitely recognised him in his cart in St John's Road at about 4.30pm near the Cross Keys pub, which again was an important statement.

They of course had the key statement made by old Conrad Smith who passed him driving on the hill leading from the Cross Keys to Southborough, but he had first told Constable Kent that there was a child sitting next to him and then changed his story to a vague "he had something next to him which could have been a child." He probably wouldn't come across as a reliable witness in court.

Edwin was quite excited by Henry's interview with a nine-year-old lad named Fred Nunn who lived just three hundred yards from the Apted stable and often hung out there with him when not at school. He kind of hero worshipped him and liked riding in the cart helping him deliver coal and also helped out at the stable with his horse. Young Fred was also friendly with a Tom Hawkins who worked for Mr Gilham the furniture restorer opposite the yard. He had often seen Harold with a brownish and white handled knife with a pointed blade killing rabbits for Tom who didn't like doing the deed himself. He had also mentioned that the blade had two or three nicks in it. The lad was apparently proud of remembering that. This was significant as Harold had insisted he had never owned a knife when Edwin first interviewed him.

Once he had read the statement of young Fred Nunn, he decided to personally interview him again along with the teenager Tom Hawkins and anyone else at the upholsterer's who might have seen Harold with a knife. From the first moment that Edwin had seen the knife tangled in the victim's hair he knew that you did not need to be a seasoned detective to realise it's significance in discovering the identity of the culprit. Although the circumstances were somewhat bizarre, he knew that it was the key and the only other explanation was that it could have been planted to incriminate another person, but he dismissed this as implausible. It's presence was not a sight he had ever seen before in the many cases he had investigated. His initial hypothesis was that during the desperate murder act the knife was accidently entangled in the girl's hair and in the murderer's panic to dispose of the body he didn't have time or presence of mind to extricate it. It was a big mistake to make.

The Hawkins family lived in a two bedroomed terraced house at 58 St Mary's Road in Tonbridge where Tom lived with his parents just one street away from the Apted family. Tom was making a career for himself having taken an apprenticeship in the skilled trade of upholstery with George Gilham.

Edwin went first to his home address but was informed by his mother Amelia that her son was at work and directed him to the upholstery workshop at 63 Pembury Road. Edwin strolled the few hundred yards to the premises of Mr Gilham and was surprised to see it was next to the Apted stable and yard. As he entered the building he found a strong looking man of about forty stuffing a couch with horse hair. The man had his back to him, and he watched as he took handfuls of the filling and forced them into the arm of the furniture. He coughed quietly to make the man aware of his presence and introduced himself.

'Are you Mr Gilham by any chance?' he asked the man.

'I am, sir.'

'That looks like very skilled and strenuous work.'

'It is that sir. Does my back no favours, I can tell you. What can I do for you?'

'I was hoping to have a word with young Tom Hawkins if I may.'

'He's about somewhere, I'll give him a shout.'

'Before you do, I noticed that the Apted yard is next door, and you have line of sight to it. I wondered if I could ask whether you saw anything unusual on New Year's Eve?'

'How do you mean?'

'Well, more whether you saw Harold Apted at all that day?'

'I have been a friend of the Apteds for a good few years, and Harold, so I don't think it fitting I get involved. I don't think it is right and proper to speak of my friends and neighbours.'

'I am not suggesting for one moment that you spy on them but whether you happened to see Harold at all that afternoon. But you do realise this is a serious murder investigation and if you can help us in any way it would be greatly appreciated.'

'What do you want to know, anyway?'

'For instance, did you see Harold arrive or go out that afternoon?'

'Let me think. I was here 'til about seven stuffing this same old couch, I know that, because I went to my sister's house who lives next door about ten to five for me tea and I seem to remember seeing him driving into the yard.'

'But did you see Harold?'

''Fraid not. Although when I got back about twenty past five I do remember seeing a light in the stable come to mention it.'

'You didn't see him though?'

'No but it must have been 'im, as no one else uses the yard.'

'I'll call Tom for you,' said Gilham irritably ending the conversation.

Tom Hawkins came sauntering in from outside looking awkward and anxious having been prewarned by his boss that the police wanted to speak to him. Edwin noticed straight away that he was of a quiet and sensitive nature and needed careful handling.

'Hello Tom. I want a word with you about your friendship with Harold Apted. Have you known him long?'

'For about three years or so. We are not that friendly.'

' I understand you keep rabbits in your back garden. Are they your pets?'

'Kind of, but we also keep them to eat from time to time.'

'You must get attached to them then,' ventured Edwin aware that the lad appeared to be of a caring nature. 'Do you kill them?'

'No chance. I hate seeing them killed, it upsets me.'

'Does your father kill them for the table then?'

'Nah, he hates to do it as well.'

'So, who does the deed for you?'

'I normally asks Harold.'

'Really. When was the last time he did this for you?'

'I asked him a couple of days before Christmas to kill four of them for our dinner.'

'Harold doesn't mind killing them then?'

'Nah. He's used to seeing animals being killed or dead seeing as he is often in the market and knackers yards.'

'How does he kill them?'

'He uses a knife and sticks them in the neck.'

'Did he use his knife to kill the four rabbits?'

'No. He said he didn't have one so could I loan him. I couldn't find mine, so I borrowed a brown handled one from my brother Bill and I sharpened it and left it on a shelf in our kitchen. I told my ma to give it to Harold when he came to collect it, but he never did come to kill them. I had to get my next-door neighbour Arthur Pilbeam to do it.'

'So you did own one?'

'Yes. I loaned it to Harold months ago to kill some rabbits, but he never gave it back. He normally did, but this time he didn't. I thought I still had it, but until you just mentioned it I had forgotten Harold had still got it.'

'So, what did your knife look like?'

'It had a brownish white bone handle and was two bladed. One big blade and a small blade that had been sharpened many times to a point ….' Tom suddenly stopped talking, his mouth open, with a look of realisation and shock on his face. 'It wasn't the knife that killed the girl, was it?'

Edwin tried to calm him. 'So it had a sharpened point?'

'Yes. I'm not a suspect am I. I didn't kill her!' he exclaimed now visibly shaking. 'I gave that knife to Harold months ago and he didn't give it back.'

'Calm down lad, not at all, I am just trying to establish who the last person was who had it. There's nothing to worry about but I will need you to come to the police station to see if you can identify the knife.'

'Does anyone else work here who might know something to help me?' Edwin asked Tom.

'Yeh, Mr Shepherd.'

'Can you find him for me?'

While Edwin waited for Mr Shepherd he was approached shyly by George Gilham's nine-year-old son named Percy who had overheard the conversation. Percy informed him that he had seen Harold killing rabbits in the yard and said 'I was proper upset I was. They were squealing and he stabbed their necks and blood spurted out. Mother had to send me to bed, I was so sick.'

Edwin commiserated with him until Mr Shepherd arrived. He interviewed him along similar lines to George Gilham, and Shepherd explained that he went at ten minutes past five for his tea break and couldn't recollect the cart being there but when he returned at twenty to six he was sure the cart was in the yard and there was a lamp on. He believed the horse was unharnessed and he could hear Harold bedding it down and feeding it. He also added that Mr Gilham had hired Harold to deliver some furniture early next morning and he had helped carry it to the yard and load it. He maintained the cart was in the same position as the night before and he had put fresh straw in it to line it. He didn't see any blood stains while doing this.

After that Edwin left Mr Gilham's, his mind was spinning at the revelations he had just heard about the knife. If Tom Hawkins identified the murder weapon as the same one he had loaned Harold it was almost case solved. It was only a short walk back to the police station which was in the same road. Edwin was certain he had enough to persuade the superintendent to arrest Harold Apted, but first he wanted to clear up some doubts he had regarding some conflicting statements of the suspect's various sightings and movements. He was not familiar with the locations and road layout that the statements referred to, so he felt he needed to survey the area for himself. He thought the best man to show him around was Inspector Savage and went in search of him.

Thirty minutes later Edwin and the Inspector were standing outside the Cross Keys public house on St Johns Road which connected Southborough to Tunbridge Wells. They were retracing the journey Fran had taken that fateful afternoon. The pub was situated on a slight curve in the road, and they could virtually scan the whole route she would have walked. More importantly it was near this spot witnesses had reported seeing Frances climb onto a cart on her way home.

'So, Powder Mill Lane is just up there' said Edwin pointing fifty yards past the pub in the direction of Southborough, 'where Harold reckons he came down from the village of High Brooms and turned right on his way home through Southborough.'

'Correct,' agreed Savage, 'and where Conrad Smith followed him at about 4.30pm.'

Edwin turned and looked down the road towards Tunbridge Wells, 'And Fran would have been walking towards us at about the same time.'

'That's right, and the two girls have given statements to say Harold was coming up the main road from Tunbridge Wells, not down Powder Mill Lane and saw Frances getting into the cart about three hundred yards down there at about four-thirty. They both commented it was nearly dark which fits the time scale.'

'So it would seem Apted has lied about his journey as he knew exactly where he picked up the girl and wanted to make sure he distanced himself from the location.'

'And our other witness, Thomas Dean the photographer fellow, who knows Harold, positively identifies him driving up the main road but claims he appeared to be alone.'

'Apted must have picked the girl up soon after he saw him.'

'Seems that way.'

'And Julia Hollamby who lives just round the corner here in Powder Mill Lane and was walking with her sister-in-law up the main road to Southborough around the same time also saw Apted heading up the road.'

'So, we are pretty sure both the girl and Apted were in this vicinity at the same time,' stated Edwin. The two of them continued walking towards Southborough. 'How far is it from here to her house?'

'About a half mile, I would say.'

'This is what I cannot understand. Why accept a lift when its, what, another ten-minute walk. She didn't really need one at this point being so close.'

' No, it is a puzzle. Perhaps she was tired, cold, or worried as it was dark. I think it may have been raining as well. It's not well lit here and there is not much in the way of habitation.'

'You could be right. The timing worked in his favour with it being dark just at the right time to shield him. But again, the parents insist she didn't accept lifts. So why did she do it this time. It's all rather perplexing.'

'Parents do not always know what their children get up to out of their sight, but I agree there must be more to it.'

'How far past her street is Vauxhall Lane?' asked Edwin.

'About another half mile, I would guess.'

'So, when he failed to stop and let her off, why on earth didn't she shout for help.'

'Again, that mystifies me. She was in Southborough high street and there must have been plenty of people about.'

'So, somehow keeping her quiet he then continues through the town and turns off into Vauxhall Lane, parks up, rapes and kills her without leaving a trace and throws her clothes over the hedge. He may have intended to dump the body there but is disturbed by the workmen, so he has to continue up the lane and in his panic decides to dispose of the body in the pond as he passes by,' hypothesised Edwin with little conviction.

'If she bled out quickly he could have bundled her back into the cart and without most of the bloodied clothing there would be very little blood deposited in the cart. The rain may have washed away all trace of the bloody ground and from the back of the cart. He then turns left onto the Pembury Road which takes him back into Tonbridge where he is seen by our other two witnesses Dean and Roe. It could make sense,' declared Savage.

'It's all a bit fanciful for me, but the circumstantial evidence is becoming overwhelming. However, you look at it, it was a brazen thing to do, abducting a child on a main street. The only conclusion I can come up with is that she must have known him and trusted him but where on earth did she think he was taking her and what for. For crikes sake she was seven years old. I don't think we need to establish where, how and why he did it in this case. He was definitely in the area at the right time as several people have placed him there and he has constantly lied. There seems to be no motive apart from depravity and unless he confesses and tells all, which doesn't seem likely, I doubt we'll ever know his reasons.'

The two officers went back to the police station satisfied that they had seen enough. Edwin discussed the case with Styles who agreed it was time to arrest Apted for the murder. He, along with the Inspector, were required at the inquest, but he managed to get a magistrate to issue a warrant before leaving, Edwin was left to organise the arrest.

*

The first inquest hearing was opened by Thomas Buss in the Vauxhall Inn at 4.30pm three days after the murder. Edwin's presence hadn't been necessary as it was only to be a formality being so early in the case and he had so much to do. There was a large number of people eager to hear the gory details of the case; so many that not all could gain entry even though the inn was quite large. They were about to be disappointed anyway as little evidence was to be given. It was common practice to use nearby taverns for the initial hearing while a more formal location was booked for subsequent ones if required. Fran's family were present, represented by solicitor Mr E Robb. Superintendent Styles and Inspector Savage arrived just in time. Seventeen volunteers had assembled to be members of the jury and consisted mostly of the town's shopkeepers and tradesmen including J. A Brotherton the fishmonger, Harry Beckett the chemist and Thomas Larking the publican. Mr T.W Ives acted as foreman. The constant adjournments that followed made many of them wish they hadn't agreed as it interfered with their work, something they later commented on to the coroner.

The only witness was the victim's father, John O'Rourke who was understandably in an inconsolable state, described by one reporter as having the "deepest grief upon his face." After he gave evidence to what had occurred the afternoon of the murder there was a strange conversation over the weight of the parcel Fran had to bring back. Her father replied that it would only have been two or three pounds and she often brought back parcels much heavier. He was also asked if she would go off with anyone or accept a lift and he replied she was a very willing child and would do anything for anyone if they asked her, but to his knowledge she had never accepted a lift before. He described his terrible loss and that he had formally identified the body of his daughter. He broke down at the end of his testimony.

Superintendent Styles then applied for an adjournment to give them time to make further inquiries and Mr Buss offered the police until the following Saturday asking the superintendent if this was long enough. The offer was immediately accepted, but one of the jurymen pointed out that most of the jury were tradesmen and Saturday would be a bad day for them, so the inquest was adjourned until noon on Monday the 13th. This initial inquest hearing had lasted under an hour.

Due to the convoluted nature of the legal system at the time there was a succession of inquest and magistrate police court hearings held and constantly adjourned during the four weeks following the murder. Most large regional towns had magistrates with court rooms attached to the police station. The magistrates were usually prominent citizens in the community such as the mayor, council members and the landed gentry. Typical of these was the chairman of the Tonbridge bench, who was a rich London chartered accountant name Charles Fitch Kemp, who had built his dream country estate in 1866 including a huge mansion 1866 where his ten children and twelve servants lived complete with stables and kennels for the hunt dogs. He soon became involved in local politics and became a magistrate.

Local juries tended to be civic minded volunteers usually local businessmen and tradesmen; no women of course as the suffragette movement was in its infancy with women were still treated as being incapable of such important work. Grand juries at the Assizes were again mostly of the same ilk as the magistrates.

The adjournments were mostly caused by the slow nature of collecting evidence. What little testing of forensic material that was available took time to be processed; there were no handy laboratories filled with technicians and scientists that the police could call upon. They depended on Dr Stevenson in London who was in great demand particularly by the Metropolitan police who felt they had priority. It took him three weeks to produce his results which eventually proved of little consequence in the case. Such were the delays that it was nine days after the magistrates had committed Harold Apted to the next Assizes to face a murder charge before the final inquest hearing was declared arriving at the same conclusion. The same witnesses were required to repeatedly relate their evidence which was harrowing for the O'Rourke family to continually hear.

These delays only served to heighten the interest in the case and each weekend drew a larger influx of sightseers to view the locations involved and each hearing increased the clamour to be present at the proceedings. It also incited more rivalry and jealousy amongst the local and "out of town" press agencies who jostled for front row seats and fought over stories from witnesses; their behaviour a bone of contention for many. The readers though lapped it up and the telegraph office had never been so busy as reporters frantically dispatched their copy several times a day. As the weeks passed the whole situation became increasingly frustrating for everyone involved and began to have a detrimental effect on the reputation of the town and its residents. The only winners were the local businesses increasing their sales from all the visitors.

Where Det. Fowle and Insp. Savage stood outside the Cross Keys to discuss the route Harold Apted took. If he came down Powder Mill Lane and turned right as he stated he would not have passed Frances but witnesses saw her climb onto a cart further down road towards Tunbridge Wells.

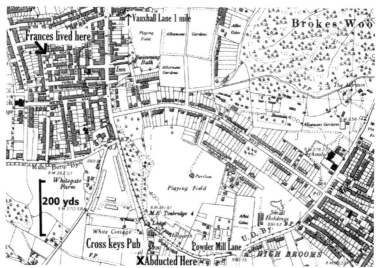

Why did Frances accept a lift when she was only half a mile, a ten-minute walk, from her home and then allow herself to be drive past her home to Vauxhall lane. [National Library of Scotland.]

6
Harold Apted Arrested

Edwin was staring out of a front window of the police station lost in thought and watching a sizeable gathering of people on the wide tree lined Pembury Road. They had been loitering all day expectantly watching for police activity. He had a serious face as he turned to Henry standing next to him and said 'I think the mood of the town is very tense don't you think, Henry?

'I agree sarge. When we were out this morning you could feel the anticipation and excitement. There were groups of people everywhere talking about the murder and we had no problem finding people yesterday eager to give us information. In fact, they came and found us.'

'Yes it's satisfying that the community has joined together to help us find the monster. They want action and the murderer apprehended double quick and that's exactly what we are going to do,' Edwin said as he turned and headed for the corridor.

'Are we going to arrest and charge Apted now?' asked Henry excitedly, 'we must have enough circumstantial evidence surely.'

'Yes, you'll be pleased to know I have a warrant in my pocket as we speak. Standby for the fireworks once we have arrested him.'

'I can't wait,' replied Henry cheerfully as he followed Edwin down the corridor.

It was 6pm when the two officers went outside and got into a waiting cab and at a fast trot headed down the street in the gloom of the gas street lamps. They marched up to the front door of 69 Woodside Rd breathing heavily in anticipation and knocked loudly. This time it was Harold

AHarold who answered and not his father. He stood in the doorway staring vacantly at the officers.

'Harold Apted I must ask you to accompany us to Tonbridge police station.' Harold made no comment but just stared at the two officers as Edwin continued, 'I am arresting you on suspicion of being involved in the wilful murder of Frances Eliza O'Rourke aged seven and a half years by stabbing her in the neck with a knife at Vauxhall Lane in the Parish of Tonbridge on the evening of the 31st. December 1901. You are not bound to say anything tending to criminate yourself and that anything you say may be used against you.'

In 1902, when arresting a suspect there was no official requirement for a police officer to caution or say anything to the alleged culprit, but it was common practice for them to give some form of a warning similar to Edwin's before the accused made any kind of comment or made a formal statement. Alternatively, the officer could just read out the details on the warrant if he had one or just tell the person why they were being arrested.

'I told you. I never came that way home. I know nothing about it,' replied a dazed Harold.

Harold's shocked parents appeared behind him having heard the commotion and they were soon joined by Charlie the brother who asked, 'what on earth is going on father?'

'Your brother is being arrested for murder,' snarled the father.

'That cannot be,' exclaimed the shocked Charlie, 'there must be a mistake.'

'I should say so,' agreed his father, 'It is preposterous.'

'We have not accused your son of murder at present, only on suspicion as we need to ask him more questions at the station,' explained Edwin in an attempt to pacify them.

His father declared, 'I'll find you a solicitor in the morning son. He'll put an end to all this nonsense.'

They handcuffed Harold and led him to the waiting carriage and were followed by the family to the pavement who stood and watched dumfounded as the carriage door slammed and the driver shouted 'hup' making the horse jerk forward and trot down the street. His brother called out 'I'll get down to the station as soon as I can to help you.'

At the station Edwin took Harold to an office and began an interview. First he retrieved the blood-stained clothing he had taken from Harold when he first detained him on Wednesday evening and laid them in front of him.

'How do your account for the blood stain on your jacket?' Edwin asked him.

Harold bent down and peered at the jacket and replied, 'Easily, it's not blood it's red paint.'

'Looks very much like blood to me. So, tell me again Harold, which way you came home that afternoon?'

'I've already told you.'

Edwin picked up the knife which had been in Fran's hair. 'Is this your knife Harold?' he asked.

'No, it isn't. Never seen it before.'

'Are you sure?'

'Yes.'

'You're pretty handy with a knife by all accounts aren't you?'

'I wouldn't say so.'

'Well, I understand from your friends that you are adept at killing things.'

'I do people favours by killing the odd rabbit for their table and helping out at slaughterhouses.'

'How do you kill the rabbits Harold?'

'By sticking them in the neck.'

'In other words, you slit their throats. Is that correct?'

'Yes.'

'When we last spoke, you said you never owned a knife in your life.'

'Did I.'

'Yes you did, but many of your friends tell me different.'

'The last time I had one was when I borrowed one. That was six months ago.'

'And what did it look like?'

'It had four blades a hole through the thick end and one of the blades also had a number and a dogs head close to the handle.'

'What happened to the knife?'

'One day while using it, I broke it, and I can't remember what happened to it.'

'A friend of yours at the market tells us a different story. He saw you with a knife in your pocket that afternoon.'

'If he did, I must have borrowed it temporarily.'

'I believe the knife found tangled in the girl's hair was yours.'

'And I tell you I do not own a knife or know anything about the girl.'

'Did you know Frances O'Rourke?'

'No.'

'Did you ever speak to her?'

'No.'

'You must have seen her around?'

'Not that I know of. I don't know what she looks like. Can I go home now?'

'I'm afraid not. You will be staying with us while we make further inquiries.'

'But I've told you I was nowhere near where the girl was found and know nothing about her murder.'

'The jury is out on that at the moment as we like to say.'

Harold was taken to the lock up to spend the night. Later that evening he was formally charged with the murder of Frances in the presence of a magistrate and the superintendent. As suspected by Edwin the news of the arrest spread very quickly throughout the town and surrounding district. Although Harold Apted had only been detained on suspicion, the anger and mood of the townsfolk was such that hordes made their way to the police station which was almost besieged. There was a lynch mob atmosphere about their behaviour. This was to prove just the beginning of the affect the murder had on the three towns, the County and the nation.

*

Early on Saturday morning, Edwin accompanied by his two detectives and a contingent of uniformed constables returned to the Apted yard in search of more evidence linking him to the murder.

'At least it's a dry day and we have plenty of light unlike the other day,' he thought to himself. It was still early, and the horse and cart was still there. 'I want this stable, and yard turned upside down and every inch searched for the missing parcel she was carrying and any sign of blood anywhere. We need physical evidence.'

All the men split up to search different parts while Edwin walked over to the cart and looked into the back. He spotted a couple of dark stains on the floorboards which had not been visible on his previous visit and climbed up into the back for a closer look. He gave the wooden floor and sides a close examination. There were narrow gaps between the boarding in which he could see strands of straw or hay wedged. There was also a sizeable dark coloured stain on the wood. He got on his knees and peered at the marks. 'Could be blood,' he thought to himself.

'George, get over here will you for a minute.'

George looked up from his searching and came over.

'Get up here and see what you think of that,' he said pointing.

George clambered up, got down on his knees next to Edwin and peered at the dark coloured dried liquid stains.

'I'd say that could be dried blood, sarge.'

'Exactly what I thought.'

'Could be the girl's,' gasped George.

'You never know.'

George watched over Edwin's shoulder as he retrieved his penknife from his pocket, opened it and then carefully cut away some slivers of stained wood and then removed some strands of straw from between the planks. He held them up to the light.

'Looks like blood stains on the straw to me. And look here,' said Edwin pointing to the boards, 'more blood here I'd say.'

The two officers jumped down and Edwin looked round the yard. 'Anybody found anything,' he shouted but received no reply. He turned to the constables. 'Has anyone searched the manure heap?'

'You are joking,' came a couple of replies.

'Henry, you don't appear to be doing anything at the moment.'

Henry stared at the heap.

'I'm not asking you to do it with your hands, man. Find a spade or fork. There must be one here somewhere.'

'What am I looking for?' asked a perplexed Henry.

'See if there's a parcel buried in there or any sign of blood on the straw.'

'Seriously sarge?'

Henry quickly picked up a hay fork when he saw Edwin's scowling face. Despite the serious atmosphere it brought a smirk to everyone's faces at Henry's bad luck.

'Right,' boomed Edwin, 'The rest of you, I want this cart turned on its side.'

Again, the constables weren't sure if Edwin was being serious.

'No, I mean it. I want this damn thing on its side to examine underneath so get to it all of you.'

They looked stupefied for a moment but then jumped to the task. They pushed the cart into the middle of the yard and with a lot of grunting, swearing and exertion heaved it onto its side to the sound of crunching wood. They watched with interest as Edwin walked over to the upturned cart and closely examined the floor again. He then walked to the other side and looked at what was the underneath and found a matching dark coloured liquid stain which appeared to have seeped down through the cracks.

'Looks as though the blood or whatever it is seeped through.'

'Or was washed through if Apted scrubbed the cart and it did rain quite heavy,' added George.

Edwin used his penknife to cut away more pieces of stained wood. 'Take these from me will you and keep them safe. These will have to go off with all the other exhibits for forensic tests,' he informed George. 'And I want that cart seized and taken to the station yard to stop anyone tampering with it.'

With nothing more of interest found they left the yard.

*

Back at the station Edwin had another conference with his two detectives. 'Well, all in all, I think that was time well spent, unlike the embarrassing morning Apted had,' commented Edwin.

'How's that, sarge?' asked George.

'Dr Watts came to the station this morning and examined his private parts,' replied Edwin having difficulty keeping a straight face.

The two detectives burst out laughing despite themselves.

'Seriously,' chuckled George.

'Yes. The Doc thought he might be able to discover if he'd had intercourse recently.'

'And?' asked Henry.

'Nothing doing, it's impossible say.'

'Anyway, moving on, the blood in the back of the cart is another indication we have the right man. How are we getting on with checking his alibi. George what have you got?'

'I've spoken to Mr Semple, the butcher who owns a shop in Tonbridge High Street and a slaughterhouse at High Brooms where Apted reckons he went about a Christmas box. Says he doesn't know Apted but that on occasions he did bring calves to him. When I explained what he had told us about collecting his tip, Semple said he knew nothing about it and hadn't seen him. He then told me something interesting. He reckoned that if Harold was at St Peters Church dropping off Kemp and was heading for Tonbridge on the back road he would have passed within five streets of his shop. If he had gone on the main road he would pass the actual shop so he cannot understand why he didn't call in rather than going all the way out to the slaughterhouse not knowing if anyone was there.'

'Interesting,' mused Edwin.

'He also added that he was aware that Mr Kemp, his slaughterman had spoken to Apted about it.'

'And what has Mr Kemp have to say?'

'Well, he recollects he told Harold not to bother going to the slaughterhouse but to see Mr Semple at his shop about the Christmas box. He also said that after leaving him at the pub in the afternoon he was at the slaughterhouse until nine o'clock with all the lights on and didn't see Harold.'

'So that rules out all that part of his alibi and alleged movements then. Well done.'

'Mrs Scott is also adamant that Harold did not visit her house that afternoon as she was in and would have heard anyone knock. She said she had been buying coal from Mr Apted senior for years and they didn't normally deliver a bill.'

'Unless she was having an afternoon nap and didn't hear,' suggested George.

'Possible,' agreed Edwin quizzically.

'But Apted's father insists he told his son to deliver a bill next morning,'

'Another discrepancy there then.'

'Father covering for his son?'

'Could well be, as he has been quite hostile in the defence of his son.'

Edwin enquired, 'Anything new on dismissing his alibi and movements that afternoon and evening?'

'A pretty mixed bunch of evidence unfortunately,' replied George. 'We have the problem of the testimony of Mr Gilham and Mr Shepherd the upholsterers. They insist that Apted was back in the yard at the time we believe the murder was being committed.'

'And the timings were confirmed by the landlord Thomas Hinckley and Fred Kirby who saw and spoke to him at the British Volunteer pub near the stables at about quarter past five and vouches for him walking his horse towards the stables at five thirty,' added Henry.

'His parents are adamant he was home by ten to six. All these accounts seem to fit too neatly for my liking,' observed Edwin.

George asked, 'Do you reckon they have connived?'

'All the timings do seem too exact and convenient I have to say,' Edwin admitted.

'His new girlfriend Miss Poole has distanced herself a bit saying she only knows him slightly. I cannot understand why if on a date they only met up for just an hour, again with the precise time of seven fifteen to eight fifteen.'

'Again, corroborated by his friend Frank Adams at the bar.'

'They are all friends of his, Kisby, Hinckley, Poole, Gilham and Shepherd. You have to wonder.'

'And you don't need a crystal ball to guess that all of these will be the defence witnesses. They will have a field day with that lot,' said Edwin reflectively. 'We still need more. Circumstantial or not, it helps to build the case. The most telling evidence we have is the knife. It is very characteristic with one blade honed down to a very peculiar and distinctive long point. Many people must have seen Apted using it. We know of at least one market worker who saw him cutting some cord with it. Having spoken to Hawkins I am convinced he had nothing to do with the murder He comes over as a harmless and honest lad and is pretty petrified at the moment that he might be a suspect. Once we can confirm that the murder weapon belonged to him and was in the possession of Apted we will have a much stronger case. For that we need forensic results and identification by Hawkins of the knife, and we need to arrange for him and this lad Nunn to pick it out. I also want to try and get more confirmation on the cart. I intend to organise a line-up of carts and knives.'

'Really clever. I would never have thought of that,' said Henry slyly winking at George.

'Yeh, I can see why they made you sergeant,' added George.

'Right, enough of that. Just for that, as you're such a resourceful fellow Henry you've got the job of getting hold of half a dozen similar carts and a load of similar knives.'

'That's not going to be easy,' moaned Henry.

'That's why I have given you the job. And I've got more good news. New evidence just in thanks to Sergeant

Bates, which will be detrimental to Apted's case,' announced Edwin.

'How's that?'

'A Mr George Pethurst, who conveniently lives with his family at 58 Woodside Road almost opposite the Apted's, came into the station and reported that about fifteen months ago Apted picked up his eight-year-old daughter from outside her school and took her for a ride up Quarry Hill.'

'You're kidding.'

'No, I'm damn well not. Read the statement from his daughter,' said Edwin passing a sheet to Henry. Petley took the statement and read out loud:

'I asked Apted to let me have a ride up to the letterbox. He asked me if I had any draws on, 'I said of course.' He said, "Let me look." I said, 'I shall go home and tell my mother.' He did not pull up my clothes, nor did I. He said come down into the ditch, no one will see you. He stopped the horse and got out. He had got some calves in his cart, and I was sitting on the seat. He got down first and stood beside the horse. And then I got down in the ditch. There was no one about when he asked me to go into the ditch. He did nothing to his own clothing. I got away and left him. I then came home with a man and a boy. He did not try to stop me. He did not kiss me or touch me at all.'

'That's in the vicinity of Vauxhall Lane and the girl is the same age,' said an astounded George.

'Exactly,' said Edwin.

'It seems he may make a habit of giving young girls a lift.'

'It does seems that way.'

'And this was never taken any further?'

'Apparently not. All the father did was scold her for being late home.'

'If I was her father I would have been straight round his house and clobbered him.'

'This could have been a trial run.'

'Makes you wonder how many other girls he lured away doesn't it.'

'It would appear that our choir singing and bible reading boy is not as angelic as a lot of people think,' remarked Edwin as he left the room, 'come on lads it's time to go next door and see what the magistrates have to say about it.'

*

7
Harold Apted in court

At midday the case was brought before the magistrates at Tonbridge Police Court, adjacent to the police station. Once again the buildings became besieged by a crowd estimated by the press to number over a thousand all eager to discover the latest news and to display their outrage. Many of them had been at the Vauxhall Inn the day before trying to gain entry into the inquest. Harold had to be taken into the court and placed in the dock an hour beforehand to avoid any trouble. There were three police officers stationed at the entrance to the court where the excitement was intense, as everyone wanted to gain admission and obtain a sight of the prisoner. When the court was opened they had great difficulty in controlling what was a stampede to get in. Within a few minutes the public gallery was packed, but everyone was well behaved and stared intensely at Harold seated in the dock. The majority that failed to gain admittance remained outside not wishing to miss out on the drama.

Amongst the crowd jostling for a view of the proceedings was a young lad who unlike all those around him, who were angry and appalled by the murder, had a permanent smile on his face and was revelling in the macabre killing, finding it exciting and thrilling. Nothing like this had happened before during his short life and he wanted to make the most of the experience. The smile on his face should have betrayed him, but he went unnoticed as most people unkindly viewed him as an idiot, even a freak because of his looks and behaviour which caused some to cruelly ridicule and shun him. He had a shuffling walk and was frail for his age due to sickness and had an unusually large head which he tended to lean to one side. The tidal wave of onlookers who constantly elbowed him aside because of his frailty prevented him getting into court but it wasn't going to stop him from carrying out his plan.

There were a large number of local and national reporters present and the space allotted to them was not sufficient, so some had to occupy seats at the solicitor's tables. Harold's sister and her husband were present and seated behind the reporters. Just after noon the deputy clerk to the justices a Mr Warner and the Clerk's clerk Mr Ernest Harris together with Superintendent Styles entered and took their seats watched attentively by the congregation. Mr Sims prosecuted, representing the Treasury and Mr W C Cripps defended. The defence lawyers had been allegedly employed by a mysterious lady benefactor of means. The magistrates consisting of Mr C Fitch Kemp the chairman, Mr H Middleton Rogers, and Mr W Baldwin solemnly entered the courtroom to a hushed and expectant audience. This was the first view of Harold that most people had, and the prisoner was described by one reporter as being:

> a fresh-looking young fellow dressed in ordinary clothes, having on a short jacket, which he kept buttoned during the proceedings. He wore neither collar nor tie but had a white scarf around his neck. He stood upright in the dock and the questions he was asked, he answered in a very clear voice. After glancing round at the spectators behind him he stood facing the magistrates with his hands behind him. He was perfectly cool and took the greatest interest in the proceedings, following the evidence intently.

There was a deathly silence in the court when the charge of "feloniously, wilfully and of malice aforethought murder one Frances Eliza O'Rourke at Tonbridge on December 31, 1901," was read out. Mr Sims prosecuting said he had only had three days to prepare a case. With most of the incriminating garments of both the victim and defendant still awaiting full analysis and with the lack of time to fully interview the witnesses he asked that the prisoner should be remanded, and the hearing adjourned. He said he also required a careful plan of the locality as a great deal depended upon the times and places involved of which he had little knowledge. He informed the court that he only intended at this point to call the father to confirm the identity and the doctor to state the cause of death which they both duly did. Mr Cripps, the defence lawyer, stood and concurred with the request for an adjournment. Much to the annoyance of all the onlookers who had queued for so long to be present and hoped to hear all the gory details an adjournment was granted until Saturday 11 January, the sitting only having lasted twenty-five minutes. Harold was taken back to the station lockup by Constable Tugwell.

*

By Sunday, four days after the finding of the body, interest in the murder had reached fever pitch in the three towns and across the surrounding district. People were arriving from near and far with special trains laid on and carriages arriving from nearby towns and villages. Through morbid curiosity thousands of onlookers made their way in every type of vehicle and conveyance they could get hold of to view the pond and conjecture on exactly where the body was positioned but all they could see was the flat water. The pilgrimage to the pond began soon after dawn until the light faded to darkness in the chill of the afternoon. A great number who could not find transport trudged the two miles or so from Tunbridge Wells in the south and Tonbridge to the north with mothers pushing heavy perambulators and old folk shuffling along with their walking sticks or supported by their grandchildren. Everyone was dressed in the dark clothing of the time with long overcoats and the women with their dresses brushing the ground making a sombre almost funeral procession. It was an extraordinary manifestation of sorrow and sympathy. Every person was relishing exchanging gossip about the murder and the arrest of Harold Apted. The *Free Press* newspaper rather uncharitably described the scene as "mostly women whose usual clean-up had for once been abandoned for the superior pleasure of a gossip and a little possible sightseeing." As the days passed interest grew rather than diminished.

There were in fact many rumours circulating amongst the shocked and angry gathering mostly encouraged by misinformed newspaper articles with no foundation. There were whispers of a second man being taken into custody which did have some vestige of truth as the police had also detained a man of interest who after detailed investigation of his whereabouts was released. There was talk of the parcel she had on her being found in someone's possession which pointed to the guilt of that person. In fact, the parcel was never found. Some believed that a pool of blood had been found in a field near where the clothes had been discarded and bloody stains on a gate post with fingerprints embedded in the blood. There was even a sick accusation that Madame Tussauds had offered £200 for a cast of Fran's body and that a well-known benefactor had given the family a furnished house.

From day one of the murder the town had been flooded with correspondents, initially from the local and County rags, but within hours journalists from London newspapers and agencies hurried to the town much to the angst of their local colleagues who accused them of producing "entertaining but totally misinformed information." There was such an eagerness for up-to-date news of the murder that the main local newspaper *The Courier* printed numerous special editions during the day which sold out "as rapidly as the fast machinery turned them out." There was intense rivalry to get the best interviews and positions at the court hearings. One of the London newspaper articles described the local coroner's jury as "hordes of rustics clad in smock frocks and hob nail boots," which caused great anger and a protest to the coroner.

Mrs Apted, when approached by the London Press Agency journalist, decided to give them an interview in the hope that it would help persuade the public to view her son in a better light. Obviously it was a plea from a protective mother attempting to alibi him and she gave a description of her son's supposed movements on the day of the murder. She obviously maintained he did not commit the murder and that he got up on New Year's Eve at seven o'clock and paid visits to several Tonbridge traders he did business with completing his last delivery at 4pm. She insisted he kept a meticulous record of deliveries in a small notebook which she showed to the reporter. She believed it was to be produced by the defence, but for some unknown reason it never was. He had then headed for the Quarry Hill road which was in a completely different direction to that of Vauxhall Lane. She told the reporter he was home by 5pm and had then stabled his horse at 5.30pm when he had his tea. After that he met up with his girlfriend returning home at 8.20pm. He was tucked up in bed before 10pm.

Harold did have his own supporters and some sections of the community argued that as he had belonged to the local church Bible class and had been a chorister, he was too upstanding a lad to have committed such a heinous act. There were suggestions that the police must have made a terrible blunder in arresting him and the real villain was still out there.

*

That Sunday evening a frail sickly 15-year-old boy was in his bedroom crouched over a table painstakingly concocting a letter by the dim light shed by a flickering candle. He lived with his parents in a villa house named Fernholme in Prospect Road, Southborough. His father earned a decent living as a piano tuner and his mother doted on the lad. His name was Alexander George Laver Moore born on the 15th. September 1886. Alex was revelling in the macabre murder, and from the moment he had heard of the tragedy he had been avidly reading reports in the newspapers and had joined the crowds at the police station and court hearings trying to catch a glimpse of Harold Apted. He was looking forward to attending the funeral next day and soaking up the atmosphere. He had begun to hero worship Harold. Soon though he wasn't satisfied with just being an onlooker and his compulsion to associate himself with the event led him to take actions which were to have serious and harmful repercussions both for him and many others associated with the case.

Alex was a loner, not through choice, but because of his looks and behaviour causing others to cruelly ridicule and shun him. He had been born prematurely and the doctor who attended him warned his parents that he would not be a normal child and they would have difficulty in raising him. He was born with an unusually large head which he tended to lean to one side, and he had a shuffling walk. He suffered from ill health, tantrums and excitability and was unable to attend school until he was fourteen years old and then only for half days. At school he was unable to participate in sports, was bullied and made an outcast and many unkind people viewed him as an idiot, even a freak, but despite this he was articulate, literate and had an artistic flair. He may well have been suffering from a condition called Macrocephaly which was commonly inherited and can cause autism or learning difficulties. His parents did their best for him and loved him.

Because of his impediments and lack of social skills Alex would withdraw into a kind of fantasy world and was addicted to reading copies of the early comics like Comic Cuts, Wonder and Answers and also the "penny dreadfuls" or "bloods" so named because of their content of ghoulish murder and violence with lavish gruesome illustrations often in colour. At the time they were the equivalent of present-day video games and were blamed for causing youth violence and suicide. The stories were serialised in weekly parts of eight to sixteen pages costing a halfpenny or penny.

Alex was not only fanatical in reading them but also wanted to become an author of the stories and he would spend all his time using his vivid imagination, stimulated by the tales he had read, to write lurid stories of his own. He posted them off to editors in Carmelite and Fleet Street in London full of expectation but sadly never receiving a reply. Undaunted he continued to write but was beginning to get frustrated. He wanted to make a name for himself and be part of a sensational story like the ones he read in the comics.

When the murder of Frances occurred, and he learned all about the terrible killing he envisaged in his muddled mind that this was just like the stories he read in the journals and saw an opportunity of seeing his writing in print. So, on that evening, surrounded by his penny dreadfuls, he sat and wrote the first of what was to become a whole stream of alarming postcards to people involved in the case, taking their names from the newspapers. After several attempts he finally finished his first missive to his satisfaction and held it up to the candle to read it through aloud.

Harold Apted is not the murderer of the poor little girl. I murdered your little girl. You won't catch me as I'm off to London. Beware my curses on you. I have now a confession to make to you and to the police. You must show this to the police, for if you don't, I shall commit another murder in this district and one of your children shall be my victim. I don't care if I hang for anyone. So not the day, so not the devil himself.

He addressed it to Mrs O'Rourke with no idea of the distress and angst he was about to cause and no idea of the repercussions for him. He shuffled out of the house full of excitement and posted it in the pillar box in his street, where he had posted dozens of letters and postcards of his stories to the London publications.

Next day, postman Herbert Thomas Bennett, arrived at the box at 1pm and emptied it, duly taking the contents to the Newtown post office where it was sorted and stamped with a postmark, but it was noticed there was no postage stamp, meaning that the receiver would be forced to pay excess postage. The letter dropped through the letter box of the O'Rourke's just before they arrived home from their daughter's funeral. John picked it up and laid it on the kitchen table.

*

Illustrated Police News /British Newspaper Archive

8.
Frances O'Rourkes Funeral

Grieve not with hopeless sorrow
Jesus has felt they pain
Thy child He has found
He'll bring her back again.
Yes, the kind Shepherd found her
Laid her on his breast,
Folded His arms around her, Hushed her to perfect rest.
(Epitaph on a wreath laid on grave.)

Monday 6 January heralded in the second week of the investigation and although Edwin had made an arrest he was still under pressure to gather more evidence. It was going to be a busy and stressful day all round. George had been volunteered by Edwin to have a day in the squalor and crime that is London taking the prisoner's clothing, and other items up to Dr Stevenson at Guys hospital. George wasn't that enthusiastic and was far from looking forward to it as he was a country boy pure and simple and did not like the city. He had been up there before on cases and couldn't tolerate the noise, awful odours, dodging the heavy traffic, both on the road, and pavements and the unclean air. He always felt so dirty after a visit.

George in fact had a sizeable parcel of twenty-one articles to convey on the train consisting of several items of Frances's clothing and her boots, clothes belonging to Harold including his shirt and coat, the pieces of straw, six pieces of the cart's flooring that had been cutaway by Edwin and several hairs and fibres also collected in the cart. Once he arrived in London he caught a cab to Guys hospital to find the doctor in his lab. Doctor Stevenson was a highly experienced senior scientific analyst, who had been appointed in 1872 by the Government to aid Scotland Yard and the Metropolitan Police but his services were soon in great demand by police forces across the country making him a very busy and sought after man. His opinion was rarely challenged, and Edwin was pinning his hopes on him finding something important to the case.

The funeral of Frances was being held in the afternoon involving most of the police force to control the expected thousands of onlookers and mourners. During the morning Edwin was holding a series of identity line ups including ones for the carts and Harold's alleged knife. A lot depended on these as they desperately needed something to take to the magistrates hearing the next morning if they were to get Harold remanded.

The two detectives with the help of local constables had spent some of the weekend finding young men of similar height, age and hair colour for the line-up which wasn't easy and worse still they had tried to track down some carts that were similar. Apted's cart had been impounded at the station for several days for forensic examination. They had also begged an array of knives from police officers and various members of the public.

The two young girls, Dupond and Muggeridge were a bit spooked and nervous about the parade, but Henry had talked them through the procedure and calmed them. Edwin realised that even if the girls did identify him he wasn't sure how reliable they would be in court. Six young men were lined up while Harold was secreted between them and the witnesses were led along the line up, but to the great disappointment of Edwin none of them could positively identify him.

'You would think that at least one of them might have recognised him,' commented a frustrated Henry.

'Indeed. The darkness of the late winter afternoon hours is in his favour, and I think accounts for the difficulty in everyone identifying him,' said Edwin sadly,' let's hope we have better luck with the carts and knives.'

Youngsters Percy Gilham and Fred Nutt were both excited and daunted when individually shown the array of ten knives in front of them. It was almost like a game for them. Both the young lads immediately picked the murder weapon much to everyone's delight. Edwin knew how important this identification was as it put the knife into the hands of Harold and linked him to the body.

Then the five carts were lined up in the yard and Edwin had more luck.

'That's more like it,' said a cheerful Edwin, 'old Conrad picked out the wagon as soon as he saw it and swears it's the one. Not that we can count on that having any credence in court, but it all adds to what we have. Edwin was too busy to attend the funeral.

*

The funeral of Frances O'Rourke was timed to take place at 3pm on Monday 6th. January and she was to be laid to rest in St Peter's churchyard on Southborough Common. A large number of relatives, friends, dignitaries and others morosely viewed Frances in her coffin in the parlour of the O'Rourke home. From early morning a huge crowd consisting mainly of women, had walked as much as four or five miles from all parts of the surrounding areas to be present to witness the cortège and internment. Everyone attending did so with the feelings of a mourner. They blocked the church door in a bid to ensure a seat in the church. When Mr Edwards, the parish clerk finally opened the doors at 2.30pm he was forced to resort to help from the police to supervise an orderly flow of people by only allowing small groups at a time. It wasn't long before he had to turn people away as all seats except those reserved for the family were filled. Superintendent Styles had again foreseen this scenario and had ensured a large respectful police presence. Inspector Savage was in charge of arrangements alongside Sergeant Saunders of Southborough police, but the spectators proved to be so orderly that they were only called upon to direct the traffic. The whole route of the cortege was lined on both sides by an immense crowd numbering four to five thousand people, and this included Elm Road where the O'Rourkes lived.

Amongst the crowd was the same frail shambling young lad with a permanent smile on his face who had been at the court, eager but frustrated at not being able to get a view of Harold Apted who had become his hero.

The community had rallied round to help the O'Rourkes with the funeral arrangements and Mr Sheepwash, a local funeral director had provided free of charge a hearse and a pair of horse cabs for the family. The small oak enamelled white coffin was draped with a white cloth pall, on the corners of which the sacred monogram for the name of Jesus "I.H.S" were woven in purple. The cortege left the parents' house at 2.30pm with a large number of family members including grandparents, uncles and aunts, cousins and by special request, Mr and Mrs Jeffery, the landlords of the Ye Olde Vauxhall Inn who had taken in the body. Mr Bourdain the foreman from the tailor's shop was present representing Mr Jenkinson who had been called away to London on urgent business.

The cortege, consisting of an open hearse and six mourning carriages, made its way past a throng of onlookers to the church and all the men removed their hats and many of the women cried unashamedly. As was the tradition for high profile funerals, householders along the route closed their blinds and businesses erected black shutters. The church bell began to toll at 2.45pm adding more melancholy to the proceedings. The coffin was met at the church gates by the Reverend T Graham, the vicar and the reverend J Agg-Large one of the curate's. As the coffin was carried through the west door into the chancel the congregation who had not uttered a sound since entering, all rose in unison. Fran's parents took their seats at the front surrounded by relatives and friends and were immediately overcome with grief, particularly Frances who had to be supported. There was hardly a dry eye. Christmas decorations were still adorning the interior and seemed out of place in the sombre atmosphere.

As the vicar began the service, it was noted he was greatly moved as he had known Frances as she had been a regular at the Sunday School. The ninetieth Psalm was read at the end of the service and immediately afterwards the vicar asked to take the liberty of saying a few words before they proceeded to the graveside. He thought that he should be interpreting the wishes of the congregation who had assembled that afternoon in expressing their sympathy and regret at the tragic death of the little one they were about to commit to the ground.

The vicar told them that in his long ministry he had never conducted the funeral of a victim of such a tragedy, but while expressing the sympathy of all the mourners he was not going to dwell upon the terrible outrage. He said that the horrendous occurrence should fill them all with shame or humble them by the fact that human nature was capable of such an atrocity. What had taken place should remind them that they could not live their own lives without the guidance of the Lord Jesus Christ as without his help there were no bounds into what depths they might sink.

The small coffin was then carried to the graveside under a giant beech tree near the entrance to the churchyard close to the south door. The teachers and scholars of the Southborough Girls and Infants school had raised money for a Sicilian marble cross. It stood on a three-block base with bevelled edges with a tastefully carved spray of lilies of the valley. "In loving memory of Frances Eliza O'Rourke, died December 31, 1901, seven and a half" was inscribed in a quatrefoil panel in the arms of a cross. As the coffin was lowered into the grave Frances broke down completely and had to be escorted in a semi-conscious condition to a waiting carriage. Once the service ended the immense crowd quietly passed by the grave and inspected the hundreds of floral tributes. A sympathiser living in Brighton had even sent an artificial wreath encased in glass asking for it to be placed on the grave which was duly done.

Everyone was touched by the proceedings particularly when a tearful school friend who could not get his wreath ready in time to deliver to the house was led to the grave by his mother where he reverently laid it. It was nearly an hour before the churchyard was cleared. What marred the proceedings somewhat was a large number of souvenir sellers doing a brisk trade in memorial cards. It was well after dusk when the last mourner left the churchyard and walked slowly down the hillside.

*

On arriving home after the funeral the O'Rourkes were all exhausted and the atmosphere was that of abject misery and went early to bed. Next morning John noticed the letter on the kitchen table. They were getting ready to attend the magistrates hearing at the police station.

' I forgot that there was a letter addressed to you on the mat last night.'

'What just addressed to me. I wonder who that's from?' responded his wife.

'It's hand written and there is no stamp on it so no telling. Locally posted though.'

'That's all very strange. No stamp you say. We'll have to pay for that. How unthoughtful.'

Frances retrieved the letter and began opening it as she sat at the kitchen table. She suddenly let out a shriek which alerted her husband and began to sob with her face in her hands.

"What on earth's the matter love?' asked her concerned husband.

'Read it John, I don't believe it. What is happening?' replied his sobbing wife.

John picked up the letter and read the awful contents. The blood drained from his face, and he too sank into a chair devastated by what he was reading. It took them quite a time to recover from the shock, 'We had better take this to the police.'

'We must give it to that detective,' said Frances.

Once there they asked the desk sergeant for Detective Sergeant Fowle. He went off to find him and a few minutes later Edwin appeared.

'Mr and Mrs O'Rourke. How can I assist you. You look distressed. Has anything happened?'

The O'Rourkes were indeed distressed and were finding it difficult to speak so they passed the letter to Edwin who began reading. His eyes narrowed as he took in what was written and kept glancing from the letter to the O'Rourkes.

'I am so sorry. I cannot believe anyone could be so cruel as to send you this. It is despicable,' Edwin angrily told them. 'Be assured that we will do anything we can to find the culprit.'

'You don't think that it could have come from the murderer and Apted is not the one?'

'Obviously we will have to investigate but I am sure this is some kind of horrendous hoax sent by some weak-minded idiot.'

Edwin went up to the office he was using and handed the letter to Henry. 'Read this.'

Like the O'Rourke's, Henry said to Edwin, 'Do you think there is any truth in this and Apted's not our man?'

'All I know is that we are trying to conduct a serious murder enquiry and now we have some idiot running around playing silly buggers writing diabolical letters.'

*

On Wednesday 8 January just after midnight Constable Kemp was on night duty at the police station and was making a regular inspection of the cells when Harold started to talk to him.

'Can I tell you something?'

'If you like,' replied Kent.

'I bought a knife at White's in the High Street [Tonbridge]. I did not use it unless I stuck a rabbit for someone. I stuck one of the blades in my hand and if you look you can see the scar,' Harold told him proffering his hand through the bars.'

'So, I see, but I don't understand why you are telling me this.'

'I don't know anything about the murder, you know' Harold continued.

'Get to sleep Harold, try not to worry about it.'

'I suppose on Saturday they will either let me off or send me to Maidstone, and then to the gallows. Many innocent men are hung you know.'

'As I said try not to think about it,' said Kemp realising the lad was really depressed and not wanting him to do anything silly.

'I don't want them to stretch my neck. What we are talking about now is between ourselves,' he said sadly and turned over in his bunk.

Kemp was duty bound to make a note of the conversation which he did.

Edwin and his team continued to collect evidence for the next hearing and organised a local surveyor named Mr

W B Gray of Claremont House, Tonbridge to make a careful survey of Vauxhall Lane and to prepare a plan of all the area between Tunbridge Wells and Southborough where the sightings and events took place. This was to be used at the court hearings for the judge and jury to fully understand the timings and movements of all those involved.

On Thursday 9 January Doctor Stevenson, the eminent analyst arrived from London at the request of Mr Sims of the prosecution and made a minute inspection of the cart after which they discussed his findings. He removed more pieces of wood for further examination and collected some hairs and fibres from the floor. These proved later to be animal hairs. Mr Sims also met with many of the prosecution witnesses who had been summoned and was engaged for some time in taking their statements.

9
A Plethora of Court Hearings

The second magistrates hearing was due to begin at 10.30am Saturday 11 January, but according to the *Maidstone and Kentish Journal*, intense activity began "as early as 8.30am", when small knots of persons, including "several of the female sex" waited for the appointed hour." The chaos of the first hearing was repeated with people leaning against the court gates ready to rush in to ensure a front row seat. Such was the frenzy that when the doors were eventually thrown open, an estimated one thousand anxious people made a tremendous rush to gain entry to find a seat.

Having already witnessed large crowds at the previous hearing, Superintendent Styles had the foresight to arrange a large police presence supervised by Inspector James Savage to control them and according to *The Journal*, "had made great improvement regarding the accommodation for the Press who numbered over twenty." Despite his best efforts the police cordon the onlookers soon spilled out onto the road causing a traffic jam of carriages, cabs, traps and horse riders much to the chagrin of their superintendent. They had to be continually ushered away further down the road. Luckily everyone was mainly well behaved, more concerned with jostling to get near the door than causing trouble.

It wasn't long before the public gallery was full. People were so packed together that at one point a man fainted and there was great difficulty removing him from the court. The suppressed excitement was palpable, and everyone wanted their first glimpse of the prisoner. Those remaining outside hung around in the hope of seeing the members of each family involved in the case. The large press contingent inside the court led to some unsightly skirmishes and consternation over their behaviour particularly the London press reporters who were described as discourteous towards local representatives fighting over seating and writing facilities often elbowing out the local reporters.

The hearing began punctually, and Harold was brought in by Constable Earnest Tugwell at which point one of Harold's friends and well-wishers called out good luck and he responded, "I am certain it will be all right." Once again he was charged with feloniously, maliciously and with malice aforethought, killed and slew Frances Eliza O'Rourke at Vauxhall, Tonbridge on the 31st. of December 1901.

Harold according to press reports appeared paler and more nervous than at his first appearance and was more respectably dressed wearing a light pair of trousers, blue serge jacket and the same scarf. He glanced sharply round the court and then stood silently with his hands clasped behind his back. Again, he did not seem concerned by his predicament and stood upright in the dock and was described by one reporter as showing "the coolness which characterised him at the first hearing." He took a great interest in the proceedings and leaned forward several times to whisper to his solicitor Mr Cripps.

Edwin was the first witness to be called and explained the circumstances of the arrest and how he asked the prisoner to provide him with the clothes he had been wearing on the night of the murder which he readily complied with. He described how he examined the clothing and the cart and discovered what he believed were bloodstains. He went on to explain how he had chipped off some of the possibly blood-stained wood for forensic examination along with the clothes and thought the cart had been recently scrubbed. Harold became very animated at this point and challenged Edwin from the dock denying that the cart had been scrubbed and that the blood had soaked through and also that there was blood on the straw. Edwin asked the court for more time to continue his inquiries and for forensic tests to be carried out.

John O'Rourke repeated the evidence of his daughter's movements on the afternoon of her death as he had at the inquest. This repetition was to become a theme at the many hearings of both courts with the upsetting facts having to be told by the distraught family. He also indicated that his daughter could be mistaken for a girl three or four years older because of her height. He stated that the family had been living in Southborough for three years and recently Frances had been in the habit of going from his house to Tunbridge Wells on errands and to shop. She had only been to Tonbridge once with him. He explained that their house was not on the main road, and you had to walk down Western Road and Norton Road to get to it. He had never seen the prisoner before.

Mr Harry Leon Manning Watts MRCS, LCP. Repeated his post mortem evidence and explained that the neck wound would have caused almost instant death. He was certain the wound was inflicted by a pointed instrument and that there must have been some amount of violence used.

A further twenty witnesses who had been interviewed by the police were then called and Harold remained passive while he listened to all the evidence. The hearing lasted all day. At the conclusion of the hearing Harold asked to speak to Superintendent Styles and Edwin. He informed them that he did not wish to attend the coroners adjourned enquiry which was to take place on Monday as he had nothing to say and had heard all the evidence against him several times over. The protracted legal procedures were getting frustrating for all those involved.

*

Sunday 12. January was not a restful day for the investigating team or local police, but there were many for

102

who it was a day off. For the second weekend in a row thousands of what were described as "ghoulish sightseers" decided to make a rather morbid pilgrimage to see the hedge over which the clothes were found and the pond to view where the body had been thrown while thousands more queued and filed through the pretty churchyard of St Peter's to view the grave and its white memorial stone and to view the messages and the wilting floral tributes. This resulted again in the police having to be vigilant in supervising them. The Vauxhall Inn takings no doubt increased greatly for the day.

Harold was visited by his parents, brothers James and John and other family members in the afternoon who had tried to offer him support and advice. After they left he was taking his last exercise of the day in the yard deep in thought as though trying to come to a decision about something. Constable Kent was escorting him back to his cell when he turned to him and said, 'I wish to make a statement.'

'Do you now. You do know its Sunday and I'll need to get hold of the detectives.'

'I need to make a statement now,' he insisted.

'Alright then, I'll put you back in your cell and see what I can do.'

The constable went off in search of his seniors. It took a while, but he tracked down Superintendent Styles.

'He wants to make a statement, eh?'

'That's what he said. Do you reckon he's going to confess,' said an excited Kent.

'That would be something. You better be present with me. Find some paper and a pen.'

The two officers made their way to his cell.

'What's all this then about making a statement?' The superintendent demanded.

'I want to make a voluntary statement,' replied Harold weakly.

'You do know that anything you say may be used in evidence at any court hearing. Are you sure you don't want us to call your solicitor?'

'No, I want to do it now.'

'Alright then.' Kent passed him a pen, inkwell and paper and Styles and Kent watched over him while he wrote:

I, Harold Apted, do declare that the knife produced in court on January 11 has never been in my possession. The knife Hawkins lent me was lost six months ago. It had a hole through the thick end and on one of the had a number and a dogs head close to the handle. One day while using it I broke it, and it was mislaid, and I have never seen it since. I did not kill two rabbits seven weeks ago. It was six months ago. On December 23, Hawkins wanted me to kill four rabbits for Christmas. I said all right, but what about a knife, Tom? He then said I will let you have my knife what I've got at home. This being a four bladed knife with a white handle and the contract was settled. But after all I did not kill them because I had not got the time. But I believe if he produces a knife you will find blood on it because I have killed rabbits with it. He told Inspector Savage. that I always gave him his knife back after I had done with it, which was quite true. The last knife I ever had was a horn handled knife with four blades. All being broke and I have witnesses to prove, I have never had a knife for four months. And also Mr. [Conrad] Smith did not see me at Southboro on the 31st of December 1901. I was in front of him all the way from High Brooms and came down Hangman's and Quarry Hill. I have never been round Vauxhall Lane from Tunbridge Wells in my life. As regards the clothing, they have been worn by my brother Charlie and the knickers have been worn by Tom Hawkins. I have killed calves in them myself and have bought calves' heads from Hawkenbury for Mr. White in my cart. Signed, Harold Apted, January 12. 1902.

*

On Monday 13 January at 2pm the second inquest resumed at the Rose & Crown Hotel in Tonbridge in their large Market Room. The proceeding got off to a bizarre start when Mr Ives, the foreman drew the coroner's attention to certain remarks which appeared in *The Sun* newspaper after the previous hearing. He stood and addressed Mr Buss:

That paper sir referred to the jury as "a lot of smock frocked heavy Hobbodyhoys, who marched into the room one by one and two by two." We don't care how much they amuse their readers, and no doubt the remarks were intended for the London customers, but we don't care for them to do it at our expense. The gentleman you preside over, sir, are fairly representative of the businessmen of Tonbridge, and I am requested to ask you that if you have the power, and the representative of that paper is present in the room, that you will politely ask him to retire.

Mr Ives sat back down, and his fellow jurors nodded approval, and several patted his shoulder. In response Mr Buss stated that the remarks struck him as being uncalled for and sympathised with them. He advised they should treat them with the disdain and the contempt they deserved. He then complimented them and said the whole town of Tonbridge had every confidence in them doing justice to all concerned. He didn't think it was within his power to take any action and hoped they would be disposed to take no further steps in the matter.

This interlude reflected the deep social and class divide which existed at the time between urban folk who perceived their country cousins as somewhat backward. The matter was then dropped, and Superintendent Styles informed the Coroner that Harold was not attending through choice and so the first witnesses were called. The same evidence from the first magistrate and inquest hearings was repeated and at the end of it Mr Buss informed the jury that until they received the evidence of Dr Stevenson regarding the nature of the blood stains and further police evidence he was forced to adjourn the inquest yet again until the following Monday 20 January at 2pm. The jury were visibly frustrated at the announcement.

Later Constable Kent, on night duty was routinely checking the cells and on passing Harold's cell noticed that Harold had his head under the blanket, and he couldn't hear or see him breathing. He entered with his oil lamp and shook him, and he woke up.

'Are you alright, lad?'

Harold peered up and said, 'There is many an innocent man hung, and I don't want them to do that to me.'

Kemp later said that Harold seemed very depressed, and so made a note of his statement in his pocket book after leaving the cell.

Next morning the superintendent authorised and arranged for him to be transferred to Maidstone prison, but he was concerned at the large number of people and reporters still present in the town and thought it advisable to secretly remove him. He liaised with Inspector Savage who organised a police presence at the railway station and discussed the situation with Edwin. They formulated a plan to smuggle Harold out the back of the police station into a cab.

His removal was on a need-to-know basis to avoid any demonstration, but this is not how it played out. No doubt their plan was leaked by a constable for beer money from a reporter and so a crowd began congregating along the road between the police and railway stations, particularly by the booking office where they knew Apted would have to pass through.

Edwin and Henry had the dubious honour of escorting Harold and they had him handcuffed between them as they climbed into the waiting cab and pulled the blinds for the short four-hundred-yard journey. The gates were opened, and the cab slowly exited and headed north up the road over the railway bridge. Sneaking a look out of the blind, Edwin was disappointed to see such a large crowd in and around the booking office. But unbeknown to the spectators they were not stopping there, and the carriage picked up speed and passed them. This caused a mad rush up Barden Road to follow them, but Inspector Savage's cordon kept the mainly well-behaved crowd at bay while Edwin rushed Harold onto the platform through a side gate.

The 6.31pm train was standing there and the trio walked onto the platform and spied the stationmaster holding open a compartment door. They climbed in and Edwin again quickly drew the blinds. The train sprung into life, coughing and hissing and giving the usual shudder as it departed the station. Harold was sandwiched between the two detectives and appeared to be totally relaxed and enjoying the intrigue. He turned to Henry and asked for a cigarette who obliged, and Harold sat calmly and smoked, contemplating what life would be like in the austere prison.

Edwin glanced at him as he puffed on his cigarette and pondered why he displayed this reserved, calm and comfortable manner in public without an obvious care in the world. It did not seem normal compared with his experiences of other villains. Edwin had spent quite a bit of time with him during these journeys and at the police station and his behaviour worried him. Many conversations he had overheard and newspaper articles he had read believed this conduct was a sign of his innocence, but Edwin being of a religious persuasion felt it could show the opposite; perhaps it was a sign of guilt, a sense of acceptance of the sin he had committed.

Once Apted had been ensconced in Maidstone prison and Edwin had completed his investigations, and handed over the evidence to the superintendent, they returned to dealing with other cases across Kent. Edwin had been working on another high-profile one which had involved a journey up to Manchester just before Christmas to arrest a man accused of matrimonial fraud by inveigling large sums of money from a rich woman on the promise of marriage. The court case was eventually heard at the same Assizes as that of Apted. Edwin and his team still had the task of escorting Apted by train from gaol to Tonbridge and back for the various hearings and also to give evidence.

*

Saturday 18 January was an early start for Edwin and Henry. They were tasked with taking Harold back to the Tonbridge police court for what was to be the last magistrates hearing. They met up outside Maidstone prison at 7.30am as they were travelling on the 8.30am train and were hoping to grab a cup of tea before taking charge of Harold. It was one of those winter mornings where your breath hung in the air when you spoke.

'Good morning Henry.'

'Good morning sarge. Damn cold this morning,' grumbled Henry as he rang the bell.

'I couldn't agree more.'

'I've lost count how many times we have had to go to Tonbridge. It seems to be never ending.'

'I know what you mean, but I reckon we will be tied up there for a while longer. It's alright for you. When you get back late every day at least you can relax. But me being in charge of you so called detectives I still have reports to write for the superintendent and chief constable and stacks of other paperwork to get through.'

The small gate in the prison door opened and a warder let them in. After a big hint they got their cup of tea and Harold was brought to them. Edwin signed the release and Harold was handed over.

'How are you today Harold? You're looking very smart this morning in that overcoat. Anyone would think you were off to court,' smiled Edwin eyeing the new or borrowed dark blue overcoat he was wearing.

They had a cab waiting and for once there was no one outside the walls to notice their departure. They arrived at the station five minutes before the departure time and bundled the handcuffed Harold into a private compartment. The train was on time and arrived at Tonbridge just after 9am. Edwin was hopeful that their arrival was still a secret and as soon as the train screeched to a halt they quickly alighted and headed for the side entrance that led into Waterloo Road. As they exited they were greeted by a wall of excited people jostling to get a view of the prisoner.

'They are not stupid in these parts,' shouted Henry as they pushed through the mob assisted by some constables, 'they were well aware that Apted was due to attend court and would be arriving early this morning,'

'There's plenty more at the nick,' shouted back one of the constables who overheard.

'Thank you, for that,' replied Edwin.

They hurried into a waiting cab and again drew the blinds for all that was worth as their arrival was obviously common knowledge now. At Edwin's instruction the cab driver took a circuitous route to the police station to try and avoid any obstructions from crowds along the way. Another throng of people greeted them there, but constables opened the gates and the cab sped through giving the onlookers little time to sight the prisoner. He was hurried into the lock-up and handed over to Earnest Tugwell, the long-suffering keeper.

The court was again crowded to capacity and people had been gathering for hours such was the intense interest in the case. Styles had made sure there was a larger police presence to control them this time. He had sternly ordered six constables on pain of dismissal to make sure the pavement on the left-hand side of Primrose Hill, the main road outside the station, was kept clear as on previous occasions it had been blocked. Once the court officials were seated the superintendent gave the signal for Harold to be brought in.

He walked in with a "firm step" wearing the dark blue overcoat Edwin had admired and was otherwise "comfortably and respectively attired." One reporter noted that: "While standing in the dock he still maintained that nonchalant, stolid and unconcerned demeanour which had characterised his conduct from the very hour of his arrest. Once the charge was read he leaned back against the dock rail with his hands in his pockets, giving an air completely indifferent. His brother was standing close behind him and he turned to smile at him totally relaxed."

All the evidence from previous hearings was presented by the witnesses in particular the ownership of the knife. Mr Sims concluded the case for the prosecution and then Mr Cripps for the defence surprisingly stood and asked the Chairman of the bench, 'I should like to know whether the case will go for trial before I address you or not?'

The Chairman of the Bench said, 'We are unanimously of the opinion that the case should go to trial.'

Mr Cripps then turned to Harold had a quiet word with him and he stated, 'I reserve my defence.'

A loud murmur of surprise greeted this announcement.

The Clerk then asked, 'Do you call any witnesses?'

Mr Cripps answered, 'Not here.'

Harold was then committed for trial at the next Assizes. At the conclusion of the hearing, the Chairman made a point of congratulating Superintendent Styles, Edwin and his detective team for the 'very creditable manner in which the evidence in this terribly sad case had been placed before the court,' which was another feather in the cap for the Detective Sergeant and his department.

Straight after the trial Harold was escorted back to Maidstone prison by Edwin and Henry to await his day in court on the 25 February. During his wait of over a month he was treated like any other prisoner but was closely watched for his safety. He was allowed to take exercise along with other prisoners in the grounds, to receive visitors and allowed access to the prison library. He spent a lot of time in his cell singing hymns and verses to wile away the tedium and distract his thoughts.

Once Harold had been ensconced in Maidstone prison and Edwin had completed his investigations, and handed over the evidence to the superintendent, they returned to dealing with other cases across Kent. Edwin had been working on another high-profile case which had involved a journey up to Manchester just before Christmas to arrest a man accused of matrimonial fraud by inveigling large sums of money from a rich woman on the promise of marriage. The court case was eventually heard at the same Assizes as that of Apted. There were also distressing cases of infanticide to deal with, plus the usual robberies, burglaries and pickpocketing, all rife during the period. Edwin and his team also had the task of escorting

*

The final coroner's inquest was held at the Rose and Crown Hotel at 2pm on Monday 20 January and all the jury members were present. The final piece of evidence was finally given by Dr Stevenson in person, and he described how he had spent four days between the 6-9 January examining all the items. He had found blood marks on the left side of Harold's coat and in the lining of the sleeve between the wrist and elbow which he estimated as being possibly a week old. Also stains in a corresponding position on the shirt. There were no blood stains on Frances's knickerbockers, leggings or boots, but some on her chest protector, petticoat and underclothing. There were blood traces on the straw and wood and blood and human hair on the knife. He could only state that the blood was of mammalian type as he had no way of differentiating animal and human blood. Neither could he ascertain definitely the time of death. The coroner then ended the evidence and made a long unusually damning closing statement to the jury.

He apologised for the long and laborious inquiry which had excited more interest in the public mind than any other he had seen. He declared that a most diabolical and gruesome murder has been committed within the district of Tonbridge the likes of which has never been seen in memory of any of those present. A crime so cruel in its inception or so repulsive in the details of its execution. An innocent child was beguiled on her way home and trapped and allured away by a man, a creature bearing the resemblance of a man but one who had the ordinary instincts of a beast of prey. The law does not and cannot give to the perpetrator of the crime the agony of the mind and torture of body he visited upon his victim, but the law can give just retribution and I am sure it is the earnest wish of all present, as it is the wish of the large public outside that the perpetrator whoever he might be will meet with his doom and that the justice and punishment will be swift and sure. Your duty as a jury is to determine whether in your opinion the death of the little girl was brought about by violence, and if so, was the violence committed by any person or persons known to them. If you decide that the child died by violence then it is your duty to say whether you are able to identify the person or persons responsible for that death or otherwise you must return an open verdict. You may now retire to your verdict.

The room was then cleared, and the jury retired to deliberate. Twenty minutes later they returned. Mr Buss asked, 'Are you agreed on a verdict?'

'Yes, sir,' replied Mr Ives.

'Do you say the deceased died from violence at the hands of some person?'

'Yes, sir.'

'Was that decision unanimous?'

'Yes, sir. The jury was unanimous.'

'Did she die at the hands of any particular person?'

'Fifteen out of seventeen of us say that the child died at the hands of the accused, Harold Apted.'

'That, Gentlemen, is a verdict of wilful murder against Harold Apted.'

'Yes.'

Mr Buss thanked the jury, 'I would like in the name of the public to gratefully recognise the readiness with which you the jury came forward to render service on such an important inquiry which has occupied a great deal of your valuable time. I personally appreciate very much the intelligence you have displayed in the conduct of the inquiry and the ready grasp you have given to a great detail of evidence. The length of the inquiry and the able manner in which you have carried out your duties therefore allows me to discharge you from any similar duty for the next twelve months.'

Mr Ives then expressed the deep sympathy of the jury with Mr and Mrs O'Rourke and asked the coroner to hand to the father six guineas which they had collected between them which Mr Buss said he was pleased to do and concurred with their sympathy. Mr Ives then expressed the jury's praise of the police and the way they conducted the inquiry. Superintendent Styles replied in the name of all the officers involved by assuring the jury and the general public that he and his comrades had felt that they had only done their duty in such a melancholy and tragic event.

*

10
The Phantom Letter Writer.

News of a phantom letter writer was soon leaked to newspaper reporters who jumped on the story with headlines such as "Is the author a lunatic?" They could not believe their luck that the murder investigation was taking a new sensational twist. They were quick to telegraph the news to various agencies across the country. Alex Moore was also over the moon at the coverage they were giving him and encouraged he sat down in his bedroom to write a follow up postcard.

> This is to say once more that Harold Apted is innocent. I met him 12 months ago and when I planned to murder your child, I selected the help of Harold Apted. I got him to bring her in his cart to Vauxhall Lane, when I took her into the field, cut her throat, stripped her and Harold Apted threw her into the pond. This was how he got his clothes bloody.

The more coverage he received in the newspapers the more letters he wrote He would eagerly scan them for a mention of his latest handiwork. Emboldened and encouraged by his increasing notoriety his imagination went into overdrive and over the next two weeks he penned a succession of postcards to the O'Rourke's which became more bizarre and threatening and even invented a secret society for himself stating "I am the head of the secret society called the Seven Brotherhood. Its secret sign is deaths heads, cross daggers and spiders webs." He began signing himself the "Bloodsucker and modern vampire and devil." He drew sketches of a long dagger at the top of the page, or with a rough sketch of a revolver with a large cross depicted beneath it. In another letter to Mrs O'Rourke, Alex cruelly said she was to die by this dagger, and he also drew an elaborate picture of a tree with a branch from which Mr O'Rourke was supposed to be hanging. At the bottom of the page was a tombstone on which was scrawled

> To the memory of Mr and Mrs O'Rourke." Alex's twisted imagination was now running riot and in another he wrote "Beware. Eye for an eye. Tooth for a tooth. Vengeance is mine. I will repay. Hand for hand. Foot for foot. Go to hell. You fool. Devil, demon, curse you all. I will murder you all in your beds. Devil take you. Ha Ha Ha! I am born to do murder.

As the postcard writing intensified and with no arrest made, the press began to criticise the police for their inaction and in the Friday 17 January issue of the *Kent and Sussex Courier*, they attacked the lack of investigation and asked why when they knew all the missives were posted in the same pillar box they had not put it under surveillance. This was a fair point to which the police did not respond. Edwin and Superintendent Styles had believed the writer to be a disturbed individual wanting notoriety but not necessarily violent or dangerous and therefore should not be taken too seriously, a fact they told the O'Rourkes. In this they were eventually proved right but at the time this was of no comfort to the frightened recipients. The police were playing a waiting game in the hope that the writer would soon get bored with sending them. Priority was being given to building the murder case leaving little time to pursue a letter writer. Edwin and his two detectives did not have the time to investigate and keep a post box under surveillance as they were also responsible for pursuing cases elsewhere in the County.

By the end of January Alex was getting bored with writing to the O'Rourkes and decided to branch out by sending messages to anyone associated with the murder whose names he discovered in the newspaper reports. It was all becoming a game to him. These postcards became more exotic emulating the drawings and characters in the penny dreadfuls. His new targets included Mrs Jenner a witness, Mrs Roe the mother of a witness, Tom Doust who found the body and Tom Hawkins and Mr Dean. These all contained the same kind of rhetoric.

At one stage he decided to get money from the O'Rourkes by demanding twenty pounds from them threatening that they would all be killed the next day and insisting they send their six-year-old daughter with it: "Beware, Madam, I say. Don't take any steps against Harold Apted. I will take steps myself and have my revenge. Send one of your little girls to meet me along the Tonbridge Road on Monday afternoon, about 4pm with the sum of twenty pounds in their pocket. If not, I will murder you and your girl. To hell with you."

He followed this up five days before Apted was tried by sending a letter to John O'Rourke warning him that if he gave evidence he would return home to find his wife and children murdered and he used such "foul expressions" that both parents were "greatly unnerved." This was the final straw for the O'Rourkes who were both mentally and physically exhausted by all the events even though the police repeatedly urged them not to take the threats seriously. Not surprisingly they were actually afraid to leave their house and felt they could no longer remain there. The police assisted them in moving to a friend's house in Tunbridge Wells. Following the trial, they moved back. The couple were described as being "utterly broken in health and spirits," which ultimately prevented John returning to his work as his nerves were shot.

Again, Alex had no idea of the harm he was causing or that his actions were now in the realms of serious criminal acts forcing the police to intervene. Superintendent Styles and Edwin decided to put more effort and resources into discovering the writer, but they were hampered by the fact that they did not have the powers to interfere with the Royal Mail. They could not open the pillar box or letters without a warrant or good reason, and they had no evidence of who the perpetrator was. They decided to get in touch with the local postmaster to see if he could assist in any way. He was more than eager to help, but he required the authorisation from his superiors in London. Having got in touch with them, a Frank Oram Wood of the Secretaries' Office of the General Post Office (GPO) was tasked with finding a volunteer to investigate the matter.

Frank decided that Frederick Charles Cartwright, a clerk in the Special Investigation Branch was the right man for the job. Fred was told to travel by train down to Tonbridge from London to confer and liaise with Edwin and Superintendent Styles. At the meeting he was informed that they believed that all the correspondence was posted in Prospect Road but could not establish who was sending them. Fred was excited to suddenly be helping the police in such a high-profile case and proved to be a patient and diligent man. He had to be, as eventually he spent an almost lone vigil of 18 days between February 5 to 22 watching the box. His first action was to make sure any future letters were intercepted and not delivered.

At first he loitered in the street, but when this proved impractical due to the inclement weather, the ever-astute Fred noticed that the box was overlooked by the parsonage where the curate, the Reverend Agg Large resided. The Reverend willingly allowed Fred to occupy a bedroom overlooking the box. Fred installed himself and his spirits were upheld with copious cups of tea and cake. Frank

Wood, his boss in London, took charge of the covert operation and kept in close contact by visiting Fred on a regular basis.

The first week of vigilance proved unsuccessful as although he saw dozens of people posting correspondence he couldn't pinpoint any individual acting suspiciously or posting daily items. But this all changed on Thursday 13 February. At about five minutes to five Fred was standing at the bedroom window with the curate drinking tea watching a postman emptying the box when a few minutes later the two of them spotted a young lad acting suspiciously. He took some items from his jacket pocket and after looking left to right as though watching to see if anyone was about, slip them into the box. Fred on a hunch quickly laid his cup on the windowsill and asked the curate to keep watching while he rushed downstairs and out into the street. He hurried to the box, but the youth had disappeared, so he opened it with the special key and found three letters. One was addressed to the curate, another to a Mrs Rowe and the third to the editor of the popular "Answers" magazine office in Carmelite St, London. Fred marked the letters with his initials. He took the one addressed to the Reverend up to him at the bedroom window and handed it to him.

'This was at the top and is addressed to you. You had better open it in my presence.'

The curate took the letter and gingerly opened it, quickly perusing it and with a look of shock he turned to Fred, 'It's a threat to kill me and my children.' The curate sat on the bed dumfounded. 'This is dreadful.'

He handed it to Fred to read. It had a dagger, a spider's web and a sword depicted at the top and contained the following message: "prepare to die and to go to an interview with the devil, your days are numbered. Keep an eye on your children for I am watching them. The wolf in sheep's clothing. When I commence my reign of terror, I shall see all Southboro sweltering in blood and gore."

'Did anyone else post anything while I was leaving the house?' He asked Fred.

'No, not at all.'

'Then its odds on it was the lad. Did you recognise him.'

'Yes, I can't believe it, but I have known him for a couple of years. He lives with his parents just a few doors down the road.'

"We need more proof, but I believe we have found our letter writer," said the beaming Fred.

Now that Fred had a number one suspect he kept an eye out for him and soon discovered that Alex was a regular. Every time Alex posted, Fred would retrieve the letters, mark them, and deliver them himself. On two occasions he found letters addressed to Emily Jenner of Meadow Road Southborough, the mother of Frederick Jenner a witness against Apted. Fred took them to her and was present as she opened them and then kept them as evidence. There were also letters addressed to the editors of certain weekly halfpenny papers. These were very naïve like this one written to the Answers magazine: "Dear Sir, I hope you would accept two or three jokes. I've tried my hand at one which is copied from Sherlock Holmes. If you don't accept the rest, I hope you have this one, because it is best of all. If it ought to be typewritten, tell me. yours truly Alex Moore."

The letters addressed to the editors would be collected by Frank Wood and taken to them to be opened in his presence. All gave the addressee as Fernholme, Prospect Rd Southborough and were of the same handwriting as the threatening letters.

Finally on Saturday 22 February, Fred spotted Alex heading home along Speldhurst Road and approached the lad in a kindly way striking up a conversation with him. He was really getting into his role as a detective. After talking about the weather, the conversation turned to the Apted trial and then the threatening letters.

Alex asked Fred, 'Have you heard of the remarkable threatening letters?'

'I'm afraid I haven't.'

'The witnesses at the trial all received them after the first trial.'

'Really. I do think I read something about them in the newspapers.' Fred added.

'So did I,' said an excited Alex. 'I reckon they were a hoax.'

'But why would someone do that, do you think?'

'To scare them of course.'

'That doesn't seem right.'

'I heard a postman found a bundle of postcards in the pillar box where I live, and someone jumped out at him and frightened him.'

'Really that must have been scary.'

'Yeh, they reckon the writer must be very dangerous,' he said almost proudly.

Alex got even more excited as they turned the corner into Prospect Road, and he pointed to the post-box ahead of them and proudly told Fred it was the one that the letters were posted in. Fred was quite surprised at how Alex spoke in a rational manner about the whole affair.

Throughout Fred's investigations he had kept in contact and met with Edwin and the superintendent on a regular basis, both of whom were impressed with his tenacious work.

'You have done great detective work Mr Cartwright. I must congratulate you. I should have you on my team,' joked Edwin.

'Anytime sergeant, it has been a pleasure working with you,' Fred replied.

'Thank you for bringing in all the correspondence. We will get it off to a handwriting expert we often use. To an untrained eye like me they all look the same, but we must have an expert handy to say so in court,' stated Edwin.

*

Early on the morning of Thursday 13 March, old Tom the gravedigger, who had lost an arm in the war, headed into St Peters Churchyard to dig a new grave. As he passed the newly erected memorial for Frances he was shocked to discover that the cross paid for by her schoolmates had been pulled down and thrown aside and a glass case containing memorabilia had been smashed. Once again word quickly spread of the alleged desecration and many locals visited the grave to show their outrage.

A few hours later at noon, Mr A Brown a local undertaker was passing the grave and noticed a luggage label with writing on it attached to the top of the cross fluttering in the breeze. He held the label and read: "I hope you are burning in hell I would cut your throat until the blood ran followed by a "jumble of the most terrible blasphemies." It was signed "The Vampire." Mr Brown intended to report it once he had finished preparing his funeral but when he walked back about twenty minutes later the label had disappeared either taken or had blown away. The Police were informed but the note was not found, and they interviewed the gravedigger who had been nearby all the time but had seen no one. Obviously the O'Rourke's family were told about the note which brought even more upset for them. Alex later admitted that he left the note but then had second thoughts and removed it. He vehemently denied desecrating the grave stone.

*

Rumours were spreading round the district and amongst the press that the arrest of the anonymous letter writer was imminent and for once they were correct. Edwin and

Inspector Savage spent Friday morning March 14 seeking to get a warrant to arrest Alex. Mr Sims the Treasury counsel interviewed several witnesses involved in tracking down Alex Moore, particularly Fred Cartwright. It was on their evidence that a warrant for his arrest was issued on two charges with several others to follow once more evidence had been compiled. At 1pm Edwin and Inspector Savage climbed into a carriage and made their way to Prospect Road in Southborough to make the arrest. They knocked on the front door, which was answered by Alex's father, also named Alexander. Edwin announced that they were police officers and wished to see his son and were immediately asked why.

'We believe he may be able to assist with our inquiries regarding the spate of recent threatening letters which I'm sure you have heard about,' the inspector informed the father.

'How on earth can he assist you. Are you seriously suggesting he has something to do with it?'

'As I said we need to speak to him to clear this matter up,' insisted Savage.

'My son would never do such a thing,' exclaimed his father, 'he is not a well boy and perfectly harmless.'

'I am afraid sir I beg to differ as we have considerable evidence pointing to your son as being the culprit.' Said Edwin bluntly. 'I have a warrant here under which I am afraid that we are now going to have to search him and your house for further evidence.'

'But this is preposterous I am not sure that I can allow that. This is my house officer.'

'I must remind you we have the power to enter without your consent, but we'd rather you cooperated and let us in.'

The father glowered at them but stood aside and led them to the parlour where Alex was sheepishly standing. Edwin had not been sure what to expect, but he was rather taken aback by the well-dressed short thin lad smartly dressed in a grey suit. Edwin could immediately see that he was sadly suffering certain physical and mental health issues.

'We will cause you as little inconvenience and stress as possible, but this is a very serious matter so please point us to the lad's bedroom so that the Inspector can search it,' requested Edwin.

While Inspector Savage went upstairs Edwin turned to Alex. 'Please raise your arms Alex and stand still while I search you. Don't be afraid lad, I'm not going to hurt you, just search your pockets.'

'Is that really necessary officer,' pleaded his destressed father.

'Again, sir, needs must.'

Edwin patted him down and emptied his pockets. In one in found three small pocket books which he placed on the kitchen table. He picked one up and flipped through the pages.

'I see you're an avid writer Alex?'

'I write poetry. I hope to be published one day.'

'He loves his writing,' his father said proudly to Edwin.

Edwin asked, 'do you ever read them?'

'Not often, no. He likes to keep them private.'

'Well in future perhaps you should,' suggested Edwin.

Edwin read one of the poems from the notebook out loud:

This is the midnight hour,
When churchyards yawn and graves give up their dead,
The grave yawns for you,
It is the midnight hour,
When we sit up in bed,
And our hair turns white with fright,
And our veins run cold with dread."

'I'm no judge of poetry but this seems to be a little unusual isn't it Alex?' Edwin asked Alex.

'Not really,' answered Alex.

'Right little poet we got here, eh Edwin?' said Inspector Savage with a smirk as he came down the stairs with a pile of comics in his hand. 'Look what I've found in his bedroom Edwin. Loads of those damn penny horribles. You can see where he gets his imagination from,' he continued passing them to Edwin to peruse.

The Inspector then went into the sitting room and returned a few minutes later. 'More of his handiwork on top of the piano and all signed by Alex stating they are his own composition and in his own handwriting. There is even a tradesman's circular with his scary sketches scribbled all over it. Blood and gore everywhere.'

'I think we have enough don't you think?' stated Edwin.

'I think we have more than enough to charge young Alex here on several more counts,' agreed Savage.

Edwin turned to Alex and said, 'Alexander George Laver Moore I am arresting you in connection with the desecration of the grave of Frances O'Rourke and on suspicion of sending a threatening letter to murder the Reverend Agg-Large curate of Southborough. I must caution that you are not bound to say anything tending to criminate yourself and that anything you might say may be used against you. Do you wish to say anything?' Surprisingly Alex resolutely replied as though he was acting a story,.

'It's a tissue of lies. I had nothing to do with the letter writing.'

Edwin then turned to his father. 'I'm afraid he must come down to the police station with us and you should come as well,' Turning back to Alex Edwin continued, 'I doubt whether you realise the trouble you are in and harm you have caused to so many people.'

Edwin and the Inspector escorted Alex and his father to the waiting carriage and took them straight to the police station court where Mr Frank East, magistrate was waiting for them. He witnessed Edwin formerly charge Alex. The press had got wind of the arrest and were also waiting outside the court but were refused entry much to their chagrin.

All the literature from the house and the dozens of postcards and letters, poems and stories sent to the comic editors in London were passed on to a well-known hand-wring expert named Thomas Henry Gurrin, often used by the police as an expert witness. He had many years' experience having been retained by the British government. He first compared the handwriting of the poems in the notebooks found by Edwin on Alex with the letters and postcards seized by Fred. Mr Gurrin confirmed that they were all written by the same hand ,"undoubtably, every one of them" he stated. He also pointed out that the writer had misspelt the word signed in every letter spelling it with a missing "n" as "siged" and that the composition of the poetry verses were identical.

Later in the day a pathetic looking Alex appeared before the magistrates at the Tonbridge Police Court with the police having enough evidence to charge him under a warrant for sending letters threatening to murder the Reverend John Agg Large. Their inquiries were on going and they informed the magistrates that they would be bringing other charges at a later date. No evidence was given, and the accused was remanded in custody until Tuesday 18 March which was coincidentally the day of Harold Apted's hanging.

At one point some were of the opinion that poor Alex may have been an accessory or even the murderer of Frances O'Rourke. Alfred Hardie, Barrister at law of Sale House, Tonbridge wrote to the Home Secretary asking for a few days reprieve for Harold Apted until Alex's possible involvement in the O'Rourke murder had been investigated and his case heard. He stated that as Alex had the "potentialities of a criminal lunatic," lived near the murdered girl and probably knew her, he should have his house searched for the missing parcel."

A bewildered Alex was led down to the cells where he was to remain for the next five days. He couldn't understand what he thought was just a prank and an adventure had resulted in him being incarcerated. In his muddled brain he had felt he had not caused anyone any harm. Unfortunately for him all the other cells were constantly full, and he was surrounded by drunks and petty thieves who shouted and cursed all the time. One of them called out to Alex asking, "so what are you in here for?"

Alex answered, 'I am in for writing the scandalous letters at Southborough. They are in my handwriting, but I don't remember writing them.'

The answer was greeted with laughter and derision by the other prisoners. Constable Tugwell, the lock up keeper, who had also looked after Harold Apted overheard the exchange and smiled to himself. 'Settle down lads, the young'un is frightened enough without you lot addin' to 'is worries.'

The next afternoon he was cleaning a couple of the cells to get them ready for new occupants when Alex called him over.

'Can I ask you something?.'

'Sure lad, but nothin' about your case for your sakes.'

'If I were to make a confession would it, say, be better for me?'

'I told you not to mention the case, but all I can advise you lad is perhaps, but I do not know.'

Alex curled up on the bunk and gave it some thought and then called over to Tugwell again who was muttering to himself about the mess in a cell, 'Mind I am not confessing, but who should I make such a statement to?'

Tugwell felt sorry for him and said, 'Now if you like, but be warned that anything you tell me I might have to tell in court.'

Alex thought again for a few minutes and then raised his head. 'I want to make a statement.'

'Alright lad, come on then. I'll take you to the office,' said Tugwell unlocking the cell. He escorted a subdued Alex up into the reception area found a quill, ink and paper and handed them to him.

'Take a seat there,' Tugwell said compassionately, but couldn't help adding, 'You obviously know how to write don't you?'

Alex sat at the desk and crouched close to the paper and carefully by the light of a lantern penned:

I, Alexander GL Moore, do hereby confess to having written all those anonymous letters circulated throughout the village of Southborough. But I say that I had nothing to do with breaking the cross on the grave though the label found there was put there by me. I only wanted to create a sensation or scare, and I am terribly sorry for what I have done.

*

11.
Harold Faces his Destiny

The Maidstone Winter Assizes opened at 11.15pm on Saturday 22 February at the Sessions House in County Road, Maidstone. The Assizes were special courts held to hear the most serious civil and criminal cases known as capital crimes directed to them by local County or magistrates courts and were held twice a year in what was called a "Sessions House." There were also Quarterly Session courts for other local serious crimes held in the building. Most County towns and cities in the United Kingdom had an imposing Sessions House many of which are now protected because of their artistic and architectural importance. Their use was replaced by the establishment of Permanent Crown Courts in the 1970s. They were presided over by senior judges from London. Two or more judges travelled from town to town on a "circuit" and there were seven circuits.

On this occasion it was the 63-year-old Justice the Hon. Sir Robert Samuel Wright Kt. who had the responsibility of this high profile and difficult murder case. He had arrived the previous Friday evening on the 7pm evening train into Tonbridge from London and went straight to his lodgings at Stone House in Leigh. Next morning, he travelled to Maidstone and as was tradition he was formally greeted by Alderman William Brownscombe, the Mayor of Maidstone, and a dozen council dignitaries and officials including the Chief Constable. He then left for the courthouse and entered the court at 11am.

At each Assizes a grand jury was formed which had to number at least fourteen members and no more than twenty-three, and on this occasion there was a full house. These were sworn in and were the usual mix of upper-class dignitaries and gentlemen of standing. It was their duty to consider whether there was enough evidence to commit the defendant for trial. A minimum of 12 had to be in agreement and they would declare what was known as a "true bill" for the trial to go ahead or "not a true bill," which ended the proceedings. The judge informed the jury of the charge and drew their attention to the facts and gave explanations before they retired to a room to deliberate. The jury had no hesitation declaring a true bill which didn't bode well for Harold, and they were thanked by Justice Wright. He then advised the court that the Tonbridge murder was the most serious and complex case on the calendar so he would hear it last. The other cases included manslaughter, stabbings, rapes, attempted suicides and violent robberies. It took until Tuesday before the judge called Harold's case.

On Tuesday 25 February the court was crowded and the expectation great. It had garnered great public interest because of the "tender" age of the victim, the brutality of the murder, its ghastly details and the youth of the accused. What intrigued many people including the press was that the evidence against Harold Apted was viewed by most as purely circumstantial and the details very complex. There was a large contingent of police witnesses with Edwin, Fisher, Petley, Styles, Savage, Horton, Kent, Tugwell and Castle, all meeting up in the foyer and chatting nervously in groups about what to expect that day. The prosecution and defence witnesses numbered over thirty. Edwin had already been in court the day before on his fraud case which had come to a satisfying end with a guilty verdict and a long stretch of hard labour. Edwin was hoping for a similar result with Apted. He had few failures and was proud of his record.

Every seat, bench, area of floor space and vantage point was occupied apart from the aisle which was studiously kept clear by the police and court officials. The gallery to the right of the bench was crammed full of mainly ladies whilst the front of the gallery to the left had been reserved for the large number of press. Everyone stood as Judge Wright entered and sat at 10.50am, but there was another slight delay for the eager onlookers when they had to wait for another case to be heard first. But at 11.05am their wait was over, and the Clerk of the Court cried the name "Harold Apted." A wave of emotion and pent-up apprehension washed over the crowded court. A deathly silence befell everyone, and they sat rigidly in their seats. Shafts of sunlight shone diagonally across the court as though to try and brighten the sombre proceedings. The expectation at seeing Harold was tangible.

It was so quiet that the footfall of Harold could be heard as he climbed up the wooden steps to the dock from below. He was wearing a neat dark blue serge suit with a high collar and blue and white tie. He had the air of respectability and intellect and bowed twice to the learned judge. He appeared calm and collected and looked younger than his age. All eyes were staring at him, but he seemed unconcerned and responded by looking all round at them.

Mr C F Gill, Kings Councillor and Mr Theobald Matthew prosecuted on behalf of the Treasury. These gentleman were the predecessors of the present-day Criminal Prosecution Service barristers employed by the Government to prosecute major crimes. Mr G F Hohler and Mr C M Pitman defended. The charge was read out yet again and when asked whether he was pleading guilty or not guilty Harold responded, "Not Guilty" in a "clear and firm voice." Thirty-two prosecution witnesses were called and only seven for the defence.

Being such a complex case involving many locations and timings a surveyor named Walter Grey had used a copy of the Ordnance Survey map of the district to show all the roads near the scene of the murder complete with distances and times to get from one point to another and covering all of Harold's movements prior to and after the murder. This was put to great use throughout the trial by both the prosecution and defence.

Mr Gill stood and addressed the jury and spent an hour outlining the prosecution case which was that the prisoner Apted had intercepted the young girl in St John's road and had induced her somehow to get onto his cart, drove her to Vauxhall Lane where he stripped and assaulted her. He then murdered her by cutting her throat and threw her body over a fence into a pond. Following this he drove back to his stable and carried on as though nothing had happened. There was an audible gasp from all those present when Mr Gill uttered the shocking details of the act of murder.

He pointed out that the only fact that was agreed by both sides was that Harold had left Tunbridge Wells at 4.30pm. But the prosecution alleged that he did not reach Tonbridge till 5.45pm and he had committed the murder during that period, whereas the defence upheld that Harold was in Tonbridge at 5pm going to a pub with a friend.

The whole prosecution case rested on the identification of the knife, which Apted denied was ever in his possession, but a witness who assisted him at Tonbridge market swore that he had seen him using it and other witnesses insisted that the knife was lent to the prisoner sometime before and he had never returned it.

The prosecution witnesses included Thomas Hawkins, the owner of the knife, the two young boys: Percy Gilham and Frederick Nutt who had seen Harold kill rabbits, Conrad Smith who saw the cart with something like a child sitting in it, Earnest Clarke who recognised the cart from the market, the scaffolders from Vauxhall lane, and the Hollamby's who thought they saw Frances in the cart. Then there were witnesses who rebutted Harold's declared movements including William Semple and Thomas White from the slaughterhouse and Mrs White who insisted Harold hadn't visited her. Edwin, Supt. Styles and several other police officers also gave evidence.

The defence witnesses that afternoon and evening called by Mr Hohler for the defence were mainly friends, family or acquaintances whose sworn evidence placed Harold either in the town of Tonbridge or so near to that town that it was physically impossible for him to have been in Vauxhall Lane at the time of the murder.

They included Mr Gilham who maintained that Harold and his cart was present at the yard at 4.40 pm.; Sydney Shepherd, who said he had returned from his tea break between 5.30pm and 5.40pm and had seen Harold's cart standing outside the stables; Thomas Hinckley, landlord of the British Volunteer public house stated that Harold was in his house at 5.15pm. Another witness that he saw a light in his Priory Street stable at 5.20pm, a third that his cart was outside his stable at 5.30pm. A fourth witness said he saw Harold in Tonbridge about 5.30pm returning by way of Quarry Hill road and spoke to him. Frederick Charles Kisby was adamant that Harold passed him in his cart at 5.15pm on the Quarry Hill Road, and later chatted to him at 5.30pm in the British Volunteers public house.

Harold's elderly father who was visibly nervous and was noted as trembling greatly arrived in the witness box and insisted his son was at home eating his tea at 5.30pm and that afterwards went out to meet a friend Frank Adams in the Foresters Arms pub at 6.50pm. Frank maintained that he spoke to him in the pub from about 6.50pm for 25 minutes or so when they were joined by Harold's new girlfriend named May Poole. Miss Poole testified that she was with the prisoner on the night in question from 7.15pm until 7.45pm and he seemed perfectly normal, but she added she only knew him slightly. All these statements were inconsistent with those of the prosecution that he had been seen in the neighbourhood of Vauxhall lane during this period and appeared to substantiate his alibi that he was not anywhere near the area of the murder.

Mr Gill was highly suspicious of the veracity of the defence witnesses testimonies and cross examined them at length. Their evidence was open to question as their statements fitted too neatly into giving Harold a complete alibi. There was talk of collusion as it was alleged that soon after Harold's arrest there had been a meeting at Mr Gilham's premises with Harold's solicitor, a Mr Daish, to gather statements. This was attended by Mr Gilham, Percy Gilham, Tom Hawkins, Miss Warner, Thomas Hinkley, Harold's father, his brother Charlie, Miss Poole and other possible witnesses.

Harold refused to enter the witness box to defend himself which stunned everyone present and caused many to whisper to their neighbours and shake their heads in disbelief, so it was going to be up to his lawyer Mr Hohler to address the jury on his behalf in his closing speech.

The evidential part of the trial had lasted all day and ended as one court reporter remarked as being a "tedious day's trial." The Court finally rose at 6.40pm once Mr Gill advised the case for the prosecution was ended and Mr Hohler had asked to give his closing speech next morning.

Justice Wright then turned to the jury and apologised for them having to overnight in Maidstone and added, "I am sure you will have no cause to complain of the accommodation you are being provided with, but if there are any problems, send the attendant to me and I will see what I can do to remedy the matter. I believe there may also be a drive organised for you tomorrow to clear the cobwebs."

The case resumed next morning, and Mr Hohler stood and faced the jury to give his closing speech for the defence which was basically that Harold was not in the vicinity when the abduction and murder took place and he attempted to discredit all the evidence put forward by the prosecution and said that it was purely circumstantial. He pleaded with the jury to eliminate from their minds all outside influences such as the press and rumour. They had failed to connect the prisoner with the murder in any way and had not given an indication of how the murder was committed. In fact, it was only an assumption that the cart seen in Vauxhall Lane had anything to do with it.

He then went on to review the evidence pointing out that any theory that the girl was murdered in the cart was improbable as it would have been deluged with blood. The small amount found was consistent with dead calves being carried in it. If she had been murdered on the ground at a spot in the lane, there would have been a large quantity of it, but the police had thoroughly searched the area and had not found any evidence of the murder scene. He pointed out that it was inconceivable that a person would commit such a murder on a highway at a time when workmen were returning home. He submitted that the prisoner's conduct was wholly consistent with being innocent and suggested that the veracity of the defence witnesses in regard to identification and timings far outweighed what he termed as hazy recollections of those of the prosecution. He criticised the police for not finding the package carried by Frances which they believed had been hidden or in finding the exact murder site. He then referred to the controversial evidence of the knife which originally belonged to Hawkins and which he claimed to have lost. He asked the jury whether a man who was clever enough to hide the package would leave his own knife in the murdered girl's hair. He put forward the theory that the real murderer purposely entangled the knife in the child's hair to throw suspicion on someone else.

He pointed out that the prosecution suggestion that the girl was thrown from the cart to the edge of the pond was preposterous and asked the jury to seriously consider whether the prisoner was physically capable of doing such a thing. He drew attention to the extraordinary fact that there was no blood on the right-hand side of the prisoners clothing. If the prisoner was guilty, he would have intended to conceal the stains found on his shirt and coat. He declared that no importance could be attached to the evidence of Doctor Stevenson the expert and quoted from a work edited by the Doctor himself to show the extreme difficulty of fixing the age of bloodstains.

Mr Hohler then suggested that the prosecution had made a great point of fixing the time of the murder at between five and six o'clock, when in fact Doctor Watts had, after examining the body next morning, stated the time of death was between nine and ten o'clock that evening. Mr Hohler concluded with an impassioned appeal to the jury to find a verdict of not guilty.

Mr Gill, then stood and addressed the jury for the Crown and insisted that the evidence was consistent with the death having taken place between 5-6pm and that it was abundantly clear that the child was in Vauxhall Lane in company with the man in charge of the cart. And he suggested that she might have been killed upon the approach of workmen to prevent her crying out to avoid discovery. Mr Gill quoted at length from prisoner statements pointing out the inconsistences particularly in regard to his possession of the knife and he urged the jury to recognise that the evidence for the prosecution showed the statements to be untrue. In conclusion, he said, the question was whether the prisoner was in Vauxhall Lane between 5-5.30pm, and if he was, counsel submitted that Apted was the person who murdered the child. Mr Gill then sat down with a flourish and all eyes turned to the judge.

Justice Wright cleared his throat and began what proved to be a long summing up at 2.25pm, some of which later proved controversial:

> There are many questions to be answered. We can only guess what happened to this girl, why she was stripped before she was killed, as it was plain she was, and how she came to be carried to that point; how anyone was strong enough to throw a body weighing seventy pounds over a four-foot fence. In every criminal case, if there is any part in which there is a reasonable doubt in favour of the prisoner, it is your duty to give him the benefit of it. If, on the other hand, there is no such doubts in the case, then, however painful the task might be, however much you might pity the man who was charged, you must do your duty as I have tried to do my duty and give an honest verdict according to your real convictions.
>
> There are several circumstances which told very strongly in favour of the prisoner which have been pointed out by Mr Hohler. Apparently there was no attempt whatever on the prisoner's part to make away with any of the things, which if he had been guilty, one might have expected him to try and do. There was also no evidence to show that he had attempted to get rid of any traces of blood on his clothes, nor have there been any reluctance on his part to face the officers of the law. In fact, his conduct had been that of an innocent man. It is only right that in my summing up, I must make this statement, because I must draw your attention to circumstances which place a different complexion on the gap case against the prisoner.
>
> First of all, there is not the slightest doubt that this girl, a girl of seven and a half years old and looking

older, wearing a white sailor hat with a black band round it and carrying a dark parcel, got into a cart like the prisoner's cart near the Cross Keys Inn. She got into the cart about 4.45pm. on the afternoon of December the 31 and somebody it is quite certain, instead of driving her by way of Quarry Hill Road to Tunbridge, that somebody drove her into Vauxhall Lane, where she was stripped and killed, and her body carried on. The hour of death, apparently, according to the evidence, was somewhere between 4.30pm and 7pm, so far as I can understand. It would, however, be for the jury to judge whether the medical evidence was sufficiently strong as to point to the conclusion that the hour of death was probably about 5pm.

In regard to the evidence of those who saw a cart on the afternoon, Mr Dean, who knew the prisoner, met him on the 31 of December about four hundred yards on the south side of the Cross Keys. If that was true, there is the end to Apted's story about going to Powder Mill Lane. Dealing with the evidence for the defence. I must point out. So, the evidence of Mr Conrad was hardly consistent with Mr Rose statement, who said the prisoner did not get home until 5.45pm. Mr Apted, the father of the prisoner, did not say anything that was not consistent with the statements given by the other witnesses. If the case have rested there it would have been for you to say whether you thought the prisoner was in Vauxhall Lane at that time. If he was there, then you cannot escape the conclusion that he is the man who committed the crime because no one else has been suggested. But there are other things connected with the case which you now have to consider.

There was a knife which was found entangled in the deceased child's hair. It is for you to say how far the man Hawkins was likely to recognise that this knife was the one which he lent to the prisoner. No one can suggest you imagine that anyone would throw suspicion on the prisoner by placing the knife in the girl's hair. Hawkins swore positively that this knife was his, and he mentioned the circumstances under which he lent it to the accused. The prisoner's statement in regard to the knife is that he said the only knife he had was one with a hole through it with a dogs head on it. But in his statement to the police, he said he never had a knife at all.

In another statement, he said he bought a knife of a different kind altogether. He made various statements about the knife, and it is for you to say what importance the knife is because it was either of damning importance or of no importance at all. You say you need to know if he had it in his possession to stab the girl, then there is no other way out of it. But if, on the other hand, you can find any way of saying that the knife got into the hands of someone else, and that someone else, by an extraordinary coincidence, committed the murder, that too is for you to consider. Regarding the blood, the doctors have fairly and rightly told you that they could not undertake to pronounce with certainty when the blood had been shed. Doctor Stevenson, who was an eminent and scientific person, gave the opinion that the blood in this case was fresh blood, but not more than a week old.

I have been told that there was no reason for the accused to go to High Brooms on the 31st of December. And the witness Mr Weeks has told you that the last time Apted brought their calves to the slaughterhouse was on December the 10th. In the face of that, it is difficult to see that a case is being made out in order to explain the blood on the clothing.

Concluding, I have tried to point out a number of circumstances by which you have to guide yourselves. Now let me again remind you in favour of the prisoner, that if you really have any doubts, it is your duty to give the prisoner the benefit of it. Any real reasonable doubt and all the benefit which he can drive from his behaviour being consistent with that of an innocent man. On the other hand, if you think that this murder, as he undoubtedly was committed in Vauxhall Lane and that the prisoner and his van were in that lane at the time alleged, still more if you think that it was his knife, I find it difficult to see how you can resist the conclusion that it was nobody but the prisoner who committed this crime.

The jury retired at 3.15pm to deliberate and most people remained in their seats in a nervous and tense state not wishing to miss anything, The judge had only just retired to his chamber when he was called back at 3.52pm. The jury had only taken thirty-seven minutes to make a decision. Harold was escorted back into the dock and stood surrounded by four warders. At this point, with the exception of Harold's father, those family members of Harold who were present left the courtroom unable to bear hearing the verdict,

In the completely hushed and expectant courtroom Mr Denman, the Clerk said, 'Gentlemen, are you agreed upon your verdict?'

To which Mr Whitehead, the foreman answered in a clear voice, 'We are.'

'Do you find the defendant guilty or not guilty to the murder of Frances Eliza O'Rourke?'

In an unfaltering voice Mr Whitehead said, 'We find him guilty, with a recommendation to mercy on account of his youth.'

The judge in his summing up had left the case in such a way that most people in the court had not dared anticipate the result and there was a loud murmur and some utterances of disbelief as many had not expected him to be found guilty . The judge asked the startled looking Harold if he had anything to say and he replied no. The jurors remained standing as did all those on the benches. The judge then addressed Harold.

'Harold Apted, the jury have performed the most painful duty that can fall to the lot of anyone. I think they have come to the right decision. You had an opportunity by law of explaining, if you thought fit, from the witness box, the circumstances which seem to tell too heavily against you. You were not able to avail yourself of that, and no one can doubt that the verdict of the jury is the right one.'

'Turning back to the jury he advised them, ' I will forward your recommendation for mercy to the right quarter.'

The jury remained standing as did Harold surrounded by four warders and there was total silence amongst all in the court, many of whom cast their eyes to the floor as the judge carried out the traditional act of pronouncing the death sentence by donning the black cap and black gloves:

The sentence of this court is that you will be taken from here to the place from whence you came, and from there to a place appointed for your execution and be hanged by the neck until you are dead, and your body shall be buried in the precincts of the prison in which you are confined before your conviction. May the Lord have mercy on your soul.'

And the Chaplain uttered the word, "Amen." With that the judge stood, bowed and left the courtroom. The business of the Assizes had ended. Harold appeared to accept the verdict and sentence stoically and glanced over to his distressed father before turning and stepping down from the dock. The immediate area outside the court was densely packed with onlookers and police constables had to make a passage for all those leaving. One of them was Harold's distraught brother Charlie who collapsed in a dead faint amongst the cries from the masses of press and onlookers. He was attended by Dr Watts who was following him out of the building, and he had trouble reviving him.

12
Harold Suffers His Fate

Upon the scaffold high, Harold Apted you must die,
For the wicked deed that you have done,
For the crime you did that day,
With your life, you'll have to pay.
And very soon you'll go to Kingdom Come.

It was not until early on Saturday morning 15 March that the Home Secretary Mr Charles Ritchie informed the Under Sheriff of Kent, Mr F Howlett, of his decision not to show clemency, which the Sheriff communicated to the prison Governor, Major Dundas. During the morning Harold had been visited by his parents, Charlie and John his brothers, his sister and sister-in-law plus three friends who all tried to give Harold courage and belief that he would receive clemency and informed him of all the letters of support that had been forwarded on his behalf. But as they left Governor Dundas imparted the news to Harold's family that clemency had been refused. He also had the unfortunate job of informing Harold that his execution was confirmed for Tuesday 18 March. It was a legal requirement at the time that a period of at least three clear Sundays must lapse between the date of the sentence and the execution to give the "condemned person reasonable and sufficient time to prepare for the other world." Soon after hearing the news, Harold sat down and penned a letter to his parents which was delivered to them on Sunday morning. It said:

My dear mother and father. Soon after you were gone on Saturday the governor informed me that the sentence of death is to be carried out on Tuesday morning at 8:00 o'clock. So, I want you and Dad to

143

come and see me for the last time on Monday afternoon. I would rather you came than anyone else. So, you won't disappoint me, will you, dear mother? Because I shall not feel happy if I do not see your face again. I expect this will be the death of you and dear Dad. But we shall meet in heaven if we ask God to forgive us our sins. He will surely pardon. I know, dear mother, that I didn't live as I ought to have done when I was at home with you. But I know that you will forgive me for not doing as you wanted me to. All I hope now is that you and all will earnestly pray for me and ask God to sustain you in your bereavement and that he would open my eyes to see the solemnity of my position and make me more fit for his presence. Now, dear Mother, I will pray for you and all my brothers and sisters. Give my love to all my friends at Tonbridge. I will now close with much love to you and all at home. I expect this will be the last letter I shall write to you. So goodbye and God bless you and keep you all. I remain your loving son. Harold Amos Apted. Goodbye.

*

Once the news broke that there was not to be a reprieve, the press returned en masse back to Tonbridge. A wave of excitement spread through the local communities which was eloquently captured by a *The Referee* columnist in his article The Shadow of the Scaffold after he visited Tonbridge to obtain local opinion of the execution.

There was no escaping from the local horror anywhere in the district last Sunday. The shadow of the scaffold lay across meadow and field, woodland and valley. I have not left Tunbridge Wells station many seconds before I came upon placards surrounded by groups of loiters. The placards announced special editions of the local paper on

Tuesday night. The hanging of Apted had commenced. I found the note of the impending tragedy dominant. There seemed to be very little local doubt as to the unhappy lads guilt. But the prevalent idea was that the recommendation of the jury would have induced the Home Secretary to grant reprieve. Apted's failure to go into the witness box damned him.

*

William Billington, the public executioner arrived in Maidstone on Monday morning 17. March accompanied by his brother John who assisted him with hangings. The Billington's were a family of executioners as William's father James had been a celebrated one as had his elder brother Thomas both of whom had died three months earlier. William visited Harold to conduct the rather macabre task of measuring his height and weight in order to calculate what height of drop was required to ensure it was an instantaneous death. Harold was only five feet six inches tall so William estimated a seven feet drop would do the trick.

In the afternoon Thomas and Ellen Apted, Harold's parents, along with his brother Charlie, visited him at his request. It was an emotionally charged visit as they now knew there was no hope of a reprieve and that they would lose their son in the morning. It was the last time they would see him alive. Being a devout family, they said prayers, and he solemnly assured his mother that he "possessed a clear conscience. I have no fear of death and I am quite prepared to meet my doom." He emphatically denied all knowledge of the murder to his mother and told her he "was as innocent as on the day he was born." He also declared to his brother Charlie that he had never seen Frances O'Rourke in his life. Their son appeared to be resigned to his fate and was presenting a stoic demeanour for their benefit but after saying "Good-bye" to his mother he allegedly broke down completely at their tearful farewell. That evening between six and eight o'clock he was occupied in writing letters to several of his relatives. In a letter addressed to his girlfriend May Poole, he wrote:

> My dear, I am taking this opportunity of answering your letter of the 7th inst, and I hope it will find you quite well as it leaves me at present. I see in your letter that you believe me innocent. Well, I can tell you candidly, I am the same today as I was when I was born. Is that sufficient? If it is not, I cannot say anymore. Signed Harold the 11th of March 1902 HM Prison, Maidstone.

The last letter he wrote was to his immediate family:

> My dear mother and father, sisters and brothers, It is with great pain that I write this last letter to you. It seems so hard to have to leave you so soon. But still, I hope and trust to the grace of God to spend the rest of my life in that promise land where God shall wipe away all tears from our eyes. And I hope, dear mother, that we shall all meet in heaven. You can rest assured that I have received the peace from God through Jesus Christ our Lord, who has pardoned all my sins. He, hating the sin, shall love the Sinner. Now I will say goodbye, and May God bless and keep you all, for his namesake, Amen. From your loving son. Harold Amos Apted. PS. The hymn we shall sing here at eight o'clock tonight will be Lead Kindly Light.

The prison chaplain, the Reverend M Watson, stayed with him until a late hour and later stated that Harold appeared quite penitent.

*

Execution day proved to be gloomy, damp and cloudy with a chill in the morning air as though mirroring the feelings of all those involved. The prison was disturbingly silent which only added to the ominous atmosphere. On execution days all men and women were confined to their cells. Harold woke soon after dawn having slept as well as could be expected under the circumstances and shortly before 7am he was brought a light breakfast of tea, bread and butter which according to the *Evening News* he apparently "partook heartily." The Chaplain was there when he awoke and stayed with him throughout this traumatic period. Then the chapel bell began its mournful tolling and Harold went to the chapel and took Holy communion accompanied by Mr Robinson, the prison schoolmaster and two wardens. A small group of worshippers sang hymns selected by Harold including "Lead, kindly light." The *Tonbridge Free Press* printed an expressive description of the scene from the point of view of the thoughts of those bystanders standing at the prison gates:

In the mind of the brief interval of waiting, pictures formed themselves dimly, the young murderer in his cell with a chaplain awaiting the coming of the chosen instrument of the law; a plain rough coffin standing ready to receive his body; a heap of quicklime nearby; a freshly dug grave in a bleak and bare plot of ground, the felon's cemetery, away beyond the buildings. Certain questions naturally suggested themselves, would Apted maintain the same calm stolid demeanour that he displayed in the dock, or would he face to face with death, find his remarkable fortitude gone? These questions held the thoughts of those present, but not for long.

147

The execution was timed to take place at 8am. Long before this an immense crowd numbering a thousand or more had gathered outside the huge stone walls of the prison awaiting the hoisting of the Black Flag which signified the execution was over. At 7.45am the executioner William Billington and his brother entered the condemned cell. Harold submitted quietly to his arms being pinioned. He obviously looked pale but walked with a firm step alongside the chaplain and did not need the slightest support. They were followed by William and John, then the chief warder, the governor Major Dundas and Mr Howlett, the Under Sherriff, Doctor Hoar and two representatives of the press. They walked the few yards to the red doors of the execution shed and the scaffold. He climbed up to the gallows and took his position on the drop without help and he looked down at the small group of witnesses in the courtyard below. It was noted that Harold exhibited wonderful fortitude.

At 7.56am his face was covered, and John Billington crouched and tied his legs together while William adjusted the noose round his neck. Both then stepped aside and at 7.58am William pulled the lever and Harold disappeared into the pit to an instantaneous death or as one journalist reported "was launched into eternity." Dr Hoar went into the pit and pronounced that life was extinct. As required by law the body hung there for an hour before being cut down and placed in a plain, unpainted pine coffin. The legally required brief and formal inquest was held, and the verdict arrived at. As the Black Flag was hoisted and fluttered in the breeze the crowd quietly melted away. There was no demonstration.

After the execution all the prison officials commented on Apted's cool and collected behaviour stating such conduct was absolutely unprecedented in their experience. He ate well, took frequent exercise and smoked freely, whilst a large portion of his time had been spent in reading the literature recommended by the chaplain. It was noticed that Harold had gained weight during his imprisonment up until the point he heard that clemency had been refused when his appetite deserted him. There were already murmurings that his conduct could indicate his innocence. The dreaded news that the sentence had been carried out was conveyed to the grief-stricken family shortly after 9am in the morning and poignantly it would have been his 21st birthday on the following Friday, a much looked forward to event that would now not take place.

The Tunbridge tragedy it is ended,
The murderer now has met his fate;
None can escape God's justice,
Must come either soon or late,
It was a fearful death to suffer,
To die in shame and misery,
And Harold Apted had to stand
Upon the fatal gallows tree.
*

13
The Mystery of the Alleged Confession.

Harold was convicted on thirty points of circumstantial evidence with no tangible forensic to back it up and without a confession his conviction and sentence was always going to be open to dispute. It polarised opinion into those who believed him innocent and those who thought him guilty plus a third group who had very little doubt as to his guilt but had the hope that a reprieve would prevail as the jury recommended. With the trial over much of the press were busily retrying him in their pages and many were finding him innocent. Readers across the nation and locals alike had followed the Apted trial morbidly and avidly in the special editions of the newspapers which at some stages were printed several times a day. Even before the trial had begun many people had strong opinions about his possible innocence. One reporter wrote, "Many people in Tonbridge are seriously disturbed at the prospect of the death sentence being carried out in the case of Harold Apted. All the way down the High Street, over the bridges and up the hill to the little house where his old parents live, one hears the fate of the young man talked about. It is not, is he guilty, but he may be innocent that forms the burden of discussion by many who knew him." So, was he guilty or not guilty?

All manner of conjecture was put forward to show that the crime could not have been committed by him and the real murderer was still at large. Many could not accept the premise that a five-foot six inch nineteen-year-old like Harold could have had the ability to have stripped and raped the girl, murdered her, disposed of her clothes, concealed the parcel and then driven her in a cart to the Vauxhall Lane pond. Then had the strength to throw her seventy-pound body over a four-foot fence to the edge of a pond several feet away all in the time frame of what the prosecution suggested was seventy-five minutes or as the defence claimed a mere forty minutes.

Others suggested that if he was guilty he must have been intoxicated to such an extent that he did not realise what he was doing or had done or that he had been framed and was the victim of a foul plot. The police were accused of suppressing evidence and had failed to follow up other lines of investigation. Much of it was pure fantasy such as Harold's clothing allegedly having been worn by someone else in between being seized by the police, the wrong interpretation of the cart wheel marks at the scene, the discovery of a pool of red crimson liquid possibly blood in a field and the blood-stained finger marks on a gate post. Although none of these were mentioned in court most had in fact been investigated but had been dismissed. Edwin had investigated the alleged pool of blood due to pressure from the Chief Constable and the Home Office and discovered that it was red paint that had been spilt while being used by workers to mark young trees and underwood. The fingerprints were those of the workers using the paint. There were queries over the fact that if right-handed Harold had stabbed Frances in the left side of her neck the resultant blood would have spurted everywhere but none was found on his right sleeve or clothing. The fact that the blood-soaked murder site and the parcel or its wrappings, were never discovered worried many, as did the fact that there was no significant blood found in the cart or stable yard or amongst the manure heap. And why was Harold's delivery book annotated with times not mentioned. The list goes on.

At the trial the prosecution produced over twenty witnesses painstakingly tracked down by the police who pinpointed Harold's alleged movements during the hours that the murder was deemed to have occurred. They all placed him in the vicinity of the murder and of having the victim in his cart. The defence could only produce a handful of witnesses mainly family and friends, who placed him at home or drinking in pubs, singing and enjoying himself during the same hours. Obviously Harold could not have been in two places at the same time so there had to be an explanation. There was an inference during the trial of collusion between the defence witnesses particularly as they had all met up at Mr Gilham's house to give statements to the solicitor. Mr Gilham when questioned at the trial did not answer to whether times and places had been discussed by them all while giving their statements. With the exception of Tom Hawkins who only gave evidence about the knife it would appear the others may well have perjured themselves in giving Harold a false alibi.

In his final conversations and letters to his family and girlfriend he maintained his innocence and allegedly when his brother Charlie asked him, 'Harold, are you guilty?' he replied evasively, 'I have nothing further to tell you.' He took great pains in prison to pray, read scripture and debate with the chaplain, which only added to his righteous persona even making some prison warders doubtful. They stated that his calm behaviour was absolutely unprecedented in their experience. He came across as an upright respectable son of a well thought of and religious family but was all this just an act which hid his real personality. In the last letter to his parents there was a telling sentence which again might indicate his behaviour was not exactly virtuous: 'I know, dear mother, that I didn't live as I ought to have done when I was at home with you, but I know that you will forgive me for not doing as you wanted me to.'

His behaviour that New Year's Eve may belie his real character. He obviously liked his drink judging by his pub crawl that afternoon and his loud behaviour and failure to complete his work; he appears to have had a liking for young girls and perhaps some perverted inclinations as there was at least one alleged incident of him propositioning a child. He was also a person that had no qualms in killing animals. In an interview with the *Kent Times and Chronicle*, Ellen Apted said that she and the whole family maintained their belief in her son's innocence particularly because of the way he had conducted himself since the day he was condemned to death. But she also made a telltale disclosure that some people "had an opinion that he was callous," which must have had some kind of basis. She insisted that he was of a retiring disposition and yet he was not adverse to rowdy behaviour in a pub. His conduct in court and while in prison might well have been an act as he gave the impression of being a calculating person.

Mothers will always be proud and supportive of their sons and tend to overlook their indiscretions and Ellen was probably no different, and her judgement may have been clouded to his real disposition. All her other sons seem to have done well for themselves and Harold appears to have been the black sheep of the family unable to hold down a good job, unhappy and frustrated in his present situation. There were many clues to perhaps a tortured temperament such as his religious fervour or possible rebellion at his strict religious upbringing, his apparent detachment and lack of remorse, his innocent behaviour, his possible frustration of his home and work situation particularly as his siblings were all doing so well. There's no doubt that modern forensic psychiatrists would probably have found many psychiatric reasons for committing the atrocity. To this day it is a common misunderstanding that someone who can commit such an extremely degenerate and horrific crime must be a monster, but paradoxically many commit such crimes so that they can feel normal in the hope it will remove a sense of impotency.

But back then society and courts were not interested in the why's of a person committing a crime and in both the Apted and Alex Moore cases there were no mitigating circumstances of mental health conditions put forward. The attitude or language of the time was more that they were all callous criminal lunatics and wretches past helping; not worthy of any form of compassion or understanding, and they all needed locking away or killed. Harold's state of mind was never considered in regard to clemency.

One aspect of the trial which mystified nearly everybody was why Harold had not given evidence in the witness box and everyone agreed that this was a big mistake which ultimately sealed his fate. A *Kentish Express* reporter commented that when the average man in Tonbridge is asked whether he thinks Apted is guilty, his first impulse is to say why did he make no attempt to defend himself. Why did he not go into the box? Harold's two brothers when questioned by a reporter gave a simple reply: "He had nothing else to say. He told the police that he did not go that way. What else was there to say?" He stolidly refused to make a formal confession in writing throughout his imprisonment and maintained his innocence until the end. Or did he?

*

In the days leading up to and after his execution the press were almost fanatical in their pursuit of trying to confirm rumours that Harold had confessed, and they hounded everyone involved. This question has remained a topic of conversation and debate in many contemporary articles and accounts of the murder. The rumours began soon after the trial and the *Maidstone Journal* commented a week after the execution that they believed the judge was aware of a confession:

Though we have been unable to learn anything officially, we understand that a rumour, for which there appears to be good authority, states that after the passing of the sentence, Apted made a confession of his guilt, admitted the justice of the verdict, and said that the witnesses had spoken the truth. It is said that the fact the prisoner had confessed was communicated to the Judge before he left the town. We are, as we have said, unable to give this statement as official, but though these rumours are usually afloat after every murder trial, we have reason to believe that the rumour of the confession is substantially correct, and that there can be but little doubt of the veracity.

In a later update the editor added: "Whether the rumour is correct or not, cannot yet be known, as we are informed that, by the order of Major Dundas, the Governor of the gaol, no information is to be given concerning the alleged confession."

There was a basis to this rumour as Justice the Hon. Sir Robert Samuel Wright Kt. sat in his chamber the day after the trial and penned the following private letter to the Home Office which had an enlightening P.S. comment.

26 February 1902
Sir,
I have the honour to tender a copy of my notes of the trial of Harold Apted convicted of murder this day at the assizes. The jury recommended the convict to mercy on the grounds of his youth, but without in any way to interfere with or diminish the weight of their recommendation I am bound to say that the crime was one of the most savage and cruel within my

experience and combined rape with murder of a child of seven.
I am Sir,
Your obedient servant
R S Wright
I am informed that the convict has privately admitted his guilt.

Unfortunately the judge in his letter does not state who informed him of the confession or the reliability of the information. This "good authority" mentioned by the *Maidstone Journal* may have had something to do with a *Daily Mail* reporter, who on the same day, was enjoying a drink in the prestigious Royal Star Hotel in Maidstone, and overheard the daughter of Henry Booth Hohler, the High Sheriff of Kent telling friends that Apted had confessed to her father. Having no luck in finding any truth in the statement he contacted the Governor at 9.30pm who told him it was a lie.

The *Maidstone Journal* was also right in that the Governor was refusing to comment as a *Kent Times and Chronicle* correspondent, who was also aware of the rumour, and believing he was on the trail of a scoop, went in search of an interview with the prison governor. He later marched up to the foreboding stone prison in the dark at about 6pm and approached the warder at the gate who told him that the Governor was not present and had left instructions that no pressmen were to be admitted and no information whatever regarding that prisoner Apted was to be given.

All this press frenzy over the confession eventually reached the ears of the Home Office in London who contacted Major Dundas for an explanation about the alleged confession. Dundas sat down at 8pm the next day and wrote a private letter to Mr Murdock at the Home

Office simply stating, "Prisoner Apted made no confession" and "I told him [the reporter} it was a lie." Another letter on the 12 March, this time from the Chief Constable, Henry Warde, assured the Home Office, "There is no foundation as far as I can ascertain for any of the various stories that have been circulated about the Tonbridge murder".

The subject calmed down for a while but was reignited by an incident at the hanging. The Chaplain Reverend J.C.S Watson visited Harold on the morning of execution just after breakfast to give him Holy Communion and accompanied him to the scaffold. Two chosen reporters were present and as they departed one accosted the chaplain and asked him if Harold had confessed to him that morning to be the murderer. The chaplain replied by saying "I am not in a position to say whether he did or did not confess." This evasive response was printed in the newspapers and further fuelled the rumour of a possible confession which was heightened by a letter to the editor of the Tonbridge Free Press on the day after the execution from a churchman which explained the rules of confession and why the Chaplain made such a reply:

Provided always that if any man confesses his secret and hidden sins to the Minister for the unburdening of his conscience, and to receive spiritual consolation and ease of mind from him, we do not in any way bind the said Minister by this our Constitution but do straightly charge and admonish him that he do not at any time reveal or make known to any person whatsoever, any crime or offence so committed to his trust and secrecy, under pain of irregularity. Irregularity being the severest punishment which can be inflicted on a clergyman under the Canon law, short of degradation from his Orders.

The press continued to encourage the mystery with articles including the *Whitstable Times* who under the heading "The Culprit's Alleged Confession," stated: "Some doubt appears to prevail as to whether the condemned youth has made a confession."

I would like to leave the last word on the mysterious confession to Major Dundas, the prison Governor who sent a private handwritten letter to Mr Murdock at the Home Office dated the 24 March 1902, six days after the hanging. It reads:

> Apted made no statement [re his guilt], but I can assure you he confessed under the seal of secrecy to the chaplain [who] practically told him to. This was on the morning of the execution. The chaplain had refused to administer the communion but when he confessed he did so.

So, when no other could persuade him, it would appear that Harold's religious beliefs came to the fore, and he could not bear to die without the facility of the Holy Communion. The underline of the word "practically," seems to indicate that the Chaplain Reverend Watson was quite forceful of the rules of Communion whereby a murderer or someone conscious of a serious sin must confess to a priest and be absolved to receive it.

*

14
Afterword

Having read the Governor's letter mentioned above, the Home Office placed it in a sealed envelope on which was handwritten: "Secret, Harold Apted. Put with papers. Not to be opened except in Department." On the back was a red wax seal and the logo of the Secretary of State Home department. The letter shows that despite all the denials that Harold and his family and friends proffered he did in fact make a last-minute confession to the Chaplain and there was no miscarriage of justice as many believed. Why there was so much secrecy over the confession is difficult to ascertain as it would have been better for all concerned if the information had been made public at the time. The only reason appears to be the sanctity under the seal of secrecy which if broken would have placed the priest in a difficult position facing possible degradation or defrocking as a clergyman. But the confession somehow became common knowledge to a small group of officials.

Although we can be pretty certain of Harold's guilt, we will never know why and where he committed the crime as Harold went to his death without disclosing the murder scene or explaining how he was able to subdue Frances in order to rape and murder her. Or was that also kept secret? John and Frances never received full closure as we call it today, but perhaps were better off not knowing. To this day the murder of Frances O'Rourke and the question of guilt or innocence is the subject of various lectures, missives and local re-enactments as it had such an impact and notoriety, but it may be time to accept once and for all that Harold Apted was the murderer.

And what of poor misguided Alexander Moore? Once Apted's execution had taken place in the early morning, the community and crowds who had gathered turned their attention to the magistrates trial of Alexander Moore which perhaps aptly was conducted on the same day and was somewhat of a postscript to the whole affair. As in the Apted case, the cruel antics of Moore had attracted much public attention and disgust and great press interest which resulted in scenes at the police station reminiscent of the Apted hearings. Edwin was again in Tonbridge to be present as a major witness in the case. It was proving to be a busy time for him. Many commented that Moore appeared to enter the court with the same indifference as that portrayed by Harold Apted, but of course poor Alex had little comprehension of the seriousness of his situation even after hearing the lengthy list of offences. The magistrates clerk stood and read out the charges to the assembled court.

> George Alexander Lavor Moore you are charged with feloniously and maliciously causing to be sent to and received by the Reverend Agg-Large of Christ Church Parsonage, Prospect road, Southborough, a certain letter threatening to kill and murder him at Southborough on 19th. February; also sending letters to John Lancy O'Rourke and other persons certain threatening letters, and further with delivering, uttering and causing to be received certain letters and writings demanding from John Lancy O'Rourke, without reasonable cause certain money to wit the sum of £20 at Southborough on March 13th. 1902.

Alex leant against the rail of the dock listening eagerly to the evidence against him, smiled on occasions and even laughed at one point. He declined to ask the witnesses any questions and when charged said nothing. He may have acted differently after Mr Sims the prosecutor stated that the first charge might amount to not more than ten years and not less than three years penal servitude and on the second count not less than three years and up to life imprisonment. He then went on to explain how Fred Cartwright had painstakingly investigated the case and how his efforts had resulted in the arrest. He also described how all the missives and poetry found in the house had been sent to Mr Gurrin a hand writing expert in London who had confirmed they were written by the same hand. He then called Edwin to the stand followed by Fred Cartwright, Inspector Savage, all the postmen involved and Mr and Mrs O'Rourke. Alex's father raised the issue of his son's health and ability to comprehend his actions, but his plea was curtly dismissed by the magistrates clerk who somewhat unfairly and uncompassionately stated the court was not interested in pursuing or enquiring into his mental capabilities. Alexander Moore was remanded in custody and committed for trial at the next Quarter Assizes in Maidstone. He walked back to his cell "smiling vacantly and looking cheerful." Soon after the police court proceedings Alex asked to write a letter to his mother in what was an impassioned and articulate missive:

> When I wrote the threatening letters it was because I
> saw a chance of creating a sensation and a mystery.
> That's all; and let me assure you I had no idea what a
> serious crime it was until I got here. I have had my
> little game and now I am suffering for it. Great
> heavens, such is the web of life.

He had certainly made a name for himself and probably to his satisfaction the press had begun to refer to him as the "Vampire."

*

At the Kent Summer Assizes in July, Alex was brought up before Justice Phillimore and indicted with "feloniously

161

and maliciously sending to or causing to be received by the Reverend John Agg-Large, John Laney O'Rourke, Frances O'Rourke and other persons knowing the content thereof, certain letters threatening to kill them." The prosecution maintained that it was an extremely mischievous thing to do and that the O'Rourkes believed that the correspondence had been written by a lunatic who may have carried out his threats of murder. So traumatised were they that they had moved from their house at one point. Also, that the letters may have defeated the ends of justice by affecting the minds of the Harold Apted jury. The prosecutor held up a copy of the publication "Answers," which contained a story titled "Vengeance is mine; I will repay" which had excited Alex so much and from which he had copied text. He was unfairly and heartlessly described variously as a deformed youth and morbid creature.

The defence counsel made a great point in his mitigation of describing Alex as of weak intellect and having a craving for excitable literature; that he still had no real idea of the disastrous effects his actions caused and that previously he was of very good character. The Reverend Agg-Large who had been on the receiving end of his letters was magnanimous in giving him a character reference by saying he had known Alex for two years and had regarded him as a harmless lad not in any way vicious.

The Justice addressed Alex and told him he had done a great deal of mischief, and it was fortunate for him and others that he did not do more harm by the wicked silly letters. When passing sentence, he commented that the letters might have resulted in the acquittal of Apted so a murderer might have gone free. Luckily for Alex and his family, when sentencing the judge did appear to treat him with some compassion and recognised his disabilities when he only gave him a light punishment under the circumstances of three concurrent six-month sentences without hard labour.

*

The events that occurred in early 1901 affected the whole community for years to come but especially affected the Apteds, O'Rourkes and Moores; all respectable families caught up in the horror and scandal which blighted them through no fault of their own. The Moores valiantly did their best in caring for their physically and mentally disturbed son with no help or understanding from the local community. They too were stigmatised particularly when Alex was released from his six-month sentence. Alexander the father continued his pianoforte and organ tuning, but they moved house to 31 St James Park. Alex their son who had caused them so much heartache and trouble died in 1922 aged only thirty-six.

The health and well-being of John and Frances O'Rourke was severely affected particularly their physical and mental health. John, who had been so devoted to his daughter, suffered the most. For weeks he was continually asked to attend coroner's inquests, magistrates hearings and eventually the Assizes court repeating and hearing the harrowing evidence of his daughter's death over and over again. Not to mention the funeral, threatening letters, having to move house, identifying her body and clothes, constant harassment from the press and all the rumour mongering. This all impeded his ability to grieve, and his health quite naturally deteriorated badly even though his wife and other family members did their upmost to keep his spirits up. Perhaps he blamed himself for allowing his daughter to do these deliveries and for not protecting her like a father should.

He could not accept what had happened and ultimately had a nervous breakdown or nervous prostration and was unable to function. This resulted in him having to give up work as he was so exhausted and lethargic. Ellen his wife was also similarly affected but not to the same degree as her husband, but she could not cope with taking on his work as well as caring for her baby and other children. They were missing Fran in many ways. It wasn't long before the family's small means was exhausted, and they found themselves in a financial dilemma.

To their credit the *Kent & Sussex Courier* newspaper encouraged benevolent residents of the neighbourhood to help alleviate their distress by donating money into a fund set up by the newspaper. In a statement they pleaded with the public to be generous and said:

> No doubt the many benevolent residents of the neighbourhood will be glad to inquire into the case with a view to alleviating the distress in which the family has been plunged, and any subscriptions sent to this office will be duly acknowledged. The poverty which has overtaken the family has rendered the conduct of an anonymous letter writer particularly despicable, as these missives were sent unstamped and charged double postage.

Luckily the local and wider community were generous, but the money raised did not last long. John soldiered on, but they were forced to move into smaller accommodation at 31 Belgrave Rd. Tunbridge Wells. John became frailer and more sickly and died in 1908 aged just thirty-eight. Frances became the bread winner continuing the tailoring business from home, helped by her three girls.

The Apted family suffered in a similar way due to their youngest son's terrible actions. After the murder they had to suffer the stigma of being the parents of a monster and were shunned by many and by those who thought they must have been aware of their son's guilt. Harold's brother Charlie who had borne the brunt of supporting his brother during the trials and in prison, married and moved out leaving his parents living alone with no help for the business. Charlie spent the rest of his life still making cricket balls.

Mr Justice Wright suffered criticism in the press for his handling of the case and his directions to the jury. Some of the decisions and comments made by him during and after the trial were indeed controversial and came under scrutiny with suggestions that he did not "hold the scales of justice fairly." Particularly his comments about Harold's failure to enter the witness box to give a plausible story and substantiate his alibi. It was thought that by not availing himself of the opportunity to defend himself it might be viewed as suggestive of his guilt and influence the jury against him. *The Free Press* went as far as to state that "Mr Justice Wright's declaration that he was unfavourably impressed by Mr Apted's silence would lead tomorrow to the jury of some future prisoner surrendering their minds to so illegal and unfair prejudice."

Many legal professionals joined in with the criticism and there were doubts about the legitimacy of the actual law and the press were also quick to condemn the law as it stood. One barrister of the Inner Temple wrote to the *Daily Mail* challenging the Justice's remarks by citing the Criminal Evidence Act 1898 which "expressly states that the failure of a charged person to give evidence shall not be made the subject of any comment by the prosecution or prejudice the prisoner." He called the judge's remarks illegal and unfair prejudice. The Daily Mail's legal correspondent in their 28 February issue ridiculed the suggestion that the "Judge and jury should not draw inference and conclusions from Apted's absence from the witness box."

Even the actual law came under scrutiny. The Criminal Evidence Act which was only enacted three years earlier was perceived by many as making things worse for defendants. Judges under the Act were allowed during the course of their summing up to comment upon a prisoners reluctance to give evidence once the verdict of a jury had been given. *The Referee* newspaper stated:

> Here is the danger of the new system. Hitherto the principle of English justice, has been that it is the task of the prosecution to prove the accused persons guilt. The new system compels the accused person to establish his innocence. If he fails to give evidence for himself, the jury will take it as an admission of guilt. Had Apted told anything like a plausible story in the witness box, the jury would have acquitted him.

Many though came to the defence of the well-known and respected judge stating there was "no judge on the bench who is more scrupulously fair to the man or woman on trial before him than Mr Justice Wright. He is a supporter of the old theory that the judge should be the friend of the prisoner at the bar, watching and safeguarding his interests, and leaning in cases of doubt, rather towards him, than towards the representatives of the Crown."

The Law Times was one learned publication which came to his defence when in their editorial pointed out "that whenever a murderer is convicted on circumstantial evidence, there is the usual outcry in the press as to the inadequacy of the evidence, but no one who is not present in the court and who has not heard all the evidence can judge as to the sufficiency of it." It also backed the legitimacy of the statement made by Mr Justice Wright after the trial that he "could not doubt that the verdict was the right one." It also supported the judge's comments regarding the prisoner's refusal to give evidence pointing out these were made after the verdict, and during the trial neither by word nor suggestion was the failure to give evidence made the subject of any comment. It was suggested that "juries, like all persons, will naturally draw their own conclusions from the absence of a prisoner from the box, and no act of Parliament ever passed will prevent their doing so."

The only people who came out of the whole episode well were some of the police officers on the case. A letter to the editor of the Tunbridge Free Press extolled their good work in the matter which Edwin must have thoroughly enjoyed reading.

Dear Sir, at the Maidstone Assizes the grand jury passed a resolution drawing attention to the able manner in which three Scotland Yard detectives acted in connection with the long firm frauds by the two tailors, [an earlier case at the Assizes] but in no way did they draw attention to the conduct of Superintendent Styles, Detective Sergeant Fowle and Detective Constable's Fisher and Petley of the Kent County Constabulary in connection with the Tonbridge murder. That these officers did their duty thoroughly and well, there can be no shadow of a doubt. The manner in which they brought the perpetrator to justice of one of the foulest murders of modern times by over thirty small links of circumstantial evidence, completing a chain from which it was impossible to escape must be deserving of the highest praise. But they are not Scotland Yard officers, but men who have risen from the ranks of our Kent County Constabulary, and for neither the Grand jury composed as it was of justices of the County, nor for the petty jury to make any comment on their conduct is, I may say, regrettable, as not only would it no doubt have been greatly appreciated by the officers in question, but it would have encouraged all other officers of our police force to have followed their excellent example. It is to be sincerely trusted that some steps may be taken to show in some practical manner that their services have not been overlooked by the County in general. Yours truly. "

The letter writer would have been pleased to see that Edwin was later commended by the Director of Public Prosecutions and Henry Warde the Chief Constable of Kent for the arrest and working up of the case as was Superintendent Styles. George Fisher and Henry Petley were also commended, and Edwin was right as they both had successful careers. Four years later Edwin was promoted to be the first Detective Inspector in the history of the force and remained in charge of the Detective Department until his next promotion to Superintendent in 1911. He was to investigate many more high-profile cases during an illustrious career.

*

Det. Inspector Edwin Fowle on left talking to Supt. Taylor in 1908.
[Courtesy of Alamy Stock Photos.]

Edwin Fowle
1872 – 1944
Badge Number 267

Edwin Fowle is the central character in this series of books for good reason as he was a much acclaimed and respected police officer in his time with an exemplary and extraordinary career, but like many of his ilk has been forgotten by history. His time as a detective spanned exactly the Edwardian era and during his 42 years and 3 months loyal service to the Kent County Constabulary he was awarded many accolades collecting a police merit star and over twenty commendations.

His police career spanned the reigns of four monarchs, and he experienced the emergence of motor vehicles, extensive train lines, telephones, radio, major advances in forensic science and innovations in policing methods as well as social transformations and changes in criminal behaviour; he seems to have taken all in his stride managing to adapt to all the new challenges. He was always viewed as a rising star and rose through the ranks from a lowly constable in October 1890 to Superintendent in charge of his own division in 1911.

He was five feet nine inches tall, broad shouldered and of stout stature with a well-groomed large moustache below a substantial nose. He was described as a driven and religious man with a great sense of duty, a somewhat questioning mind and a tenacious nature, perfect attributes for a detective. He was a stickler for correct police procedure and record keeping and his superiors and the judiciary were complimentary for the way he prepared cases for court, few of which failed to get a prosecution. As a detective he was always smartly dressed, always wearing the fashionable derby hat and overcoat.

Born in 1872 to Thomas and Margaret in the small village of Preston situated between Canterbury and Ramsgate he became part of a family police dynasty as his father Thomas was also a celebrated Kent policeman who surpassed Edwin by completing 53 years' service and rose to the rank of superintendent. Two of Edwin's three brothers were Kent police officers. His elder brother Thomas rose to the rank of superintendent and his younger brother Ivo was an Inspector and one of his uncles was in the police before becoming a railway detective. They managed to boast three superintendents and an inspector in the family with an unrivalled service record which spanned a century of an incredible 165 years excluding the uncle.

He worked as a cooper in the village until he was eighteen and able to join the police. During his first six years he was posted to the Kentish towns of Gillingham, Westgate, Dartford, Ightham and Malling where he gained considerable experience. There was no real training at the time, and he learned from the "old hands." From the beginning he was perceived as having a natural aptitude for police work and particularly an ability for investigative work.

So when on the 1 July 1896 the Force had the prescience to establish a detective branch at their Wrens Court headquarters in Maidstone he was immediately picked to become one of the first three detective constables in the history of the force under the supervision of one Detective Sergeant. This tiny unit was responsible for serious crime across the County, and he helped launch and shape this new innovation. He made such an impression that four years later in 1900 he was promoted to First Class Detective Sergeant and was put in charge of the department.

In the next six years he made quite a name for himself becoming one of the most recognised officers across the

County although he made every effort to shun the press and publicity and never gave interviews he was ever in the newspapers due to the many headline cases he investigated. He was a popular officer and familiar to most of the public, judiciary, local authorities, coroners, his far-flung colleagues across the County; also to many villains. He was called upon to deal with every known class of crime whether it be murder, fraud, infanticide, robbery, hotel theft housebreaking or pickpocketing. He was sadly regularly engaged in investigating child murders prevalent in his early years which were distressing for him as a religious man.

His pet hate were all the pick-pocket gangs that frequented Kent which he pursued with a vengeance. One of his attributes was that he never forgot a face. He made a point of knowing them and they soon knew him, some of them to their cost. Such was his fixation that he could recognise all the members of the leading notorious London and Kent pickpocket gangs. Despite this the criminal fraternity had a wary respect for him and referred to him as "The Terrier."

While a detective between 1900-1911 he collected many commendations and awards. The most memorable being three headline murder cases; known as The Tonbridge murder (1901), The Tenterden Murder (1905) and the Seal Chart Murder (1908). For each one he received a commendation from the Director of Public Prosecutions (DPP) and the Chief Constable and for the Tenterden murder a police Merit Star. These three murders are all part of my *Detective Edwin Fowle Series*.

He got married on the 9th. November 1910 in St Michaels Church, Beckenham to Annie Sophia Vockins. Edwin remained with the detective department until his promotion on the 20 April 1911 to the rank of Superintendent. He was given command of the Sevenoaks

Division, "a post which he held with zeal from that day" until his retirement in December 1932. While in Sevenoaks he was known for his patience and tact and "preventing frayed tempers."

He was highly respected by the public, counsel, solicitors, magistrates and local authorities and loved by his men; encouraging them in their recreations especially cricket and rifle shooting and tutored them in first aid. Under his guidance his men played a conspicuous part assisting the injured in the disastrous 1927 Sevenoaks train crash which killed thirteen people. On retirement he remained in Sevenoaks.

He died peacefully aged 73 in Holmesdale Hospital Sevenoaks in 1944 and was buried in Greatness cemetery. At his funeral the vicar spoke of the power by which had lived and served the police force. First there was the sense of duty by which he was always exact, ready and alert to execute his work and secondly there was the maintenance of peace inspired by the source of all power, God.

The funeral was attended by family, dozens of senior officers from across the County, as well as rank and file and a large contingent of local dignitaries, friends, acquaintances and towns folk and even the local RSPCA Inspector.

*

About the Author

John Brookland is now retired and lives in Suffolk, U.K. after a long-varied career working at the sharp end of animal welfare in the U.K and abroad. Having always had an interest in social history and true crime he now researches and writes books and magazine articles on these subjects. These include the Detective Edwin Fowle series chronicling the exploits of a real celebrated Edwardian detective. He has also authored memoirs of his work helping animals in the U.K. and abroad and books on the history of department stores and the War Horses.

He also authors a popular educational animal welfare blog *www.animalrightsandwrongs.uk* commentating on international and U.K. animal issues with readers in over 70 countries. When not writing he enjoys travelling with his partner Debbie to exotic places to view wildlife and wandering the U.K. countryside.

Bibliography

National Archives, Kew, London
File HO144/791/A63233 Harold Apted
A63233 Letter dated 26 February 1902 from Justice R S Wright to Home office informing them that Harold Apted had "privately admitted his guilt."
A63233/2 Letter dated 28 February 1902 Major Dundas prison governor to Home office stating Harold Apted had not confessed.
A63223 Letter dated 24 March 1902 from Chief Constable Warde to Mr Murdock Home Office, "no truth in various stories."

Kent County Library and Archives, Maidstone, Kent.
C/PO/22/9/1 Inherited Local Force General personnel records 1869-1922)
C/PO/22/5/1 Records of Service (1857-1899)
C/PO/22/5/3 (1874-1900)
C/PO/22/5/4 (1900-1908)
C/PO/22/5/5 (1908-1920)
C/PO/22/8 Commendations
P33/10/1 Regulations and instructions to police officers 1800s

SELECTED SOURCES

British Newspaper Archive
Kent Police Museum, Faversham, Kent.
Ancestry.co.uk Census 1871,1881,1891,1901,1911,1939
Chapter Heading Poems taken from the 19th Century Broadside Ballad Trade No 29: Norfolk printings of murder and execution (4) The Gressenhall cache, part two. *mustrad.org.uk*

In total over 150 newspaper articles and references were sourced including:.

1.NEW YEAR'S EVE 1901
'Murder in Tonbridge, Date of execution' (8 March 1902) p5

'Shocking Murder of a Girl' *The Courier* (8 January 1902) p2

2.NEW YEAR'S DAY 1902 A BODY FOUND
'Murder at Tonbridge' *London Evening News* (1 January 1902) p3
'Outrage and Murder' *Manchester Evening News* (1 January 1902) p3
'News vendors offence' *Epsom Times* (21 January 1902) p4
'Shocking Murder of a Girl' *The Courier* (3 January 1902) p6

3.DET. EDWIN FOWLE TAKES CHARGE.
'A Shocking Outrage at Tonbridge. Latest Details, *Kentish Express* (4 January 1902) p4
'The Murder.' *Tonbridge Free Press* (11 January 1902) p3
A63233 *National Archives* (January 1902) Statement of George Henry Pethurst that his daughter aged 7 was propositioned by Harold Apted.

6. HAROLD APTED ARRESTED
A Light In The Lane, *Weekly Dispatch (London)* (19 January 1902)
The Tonbridge Tragedy *Illustrated Police News* (18 January 1902)

7.HAROLD APTED COURT
The Murder of a Little Girl Tonbridge *Whitstable Times* (29 January 1902)

8.FRANCES O'ROURKES FUNERAL
'Funeral of the Victim' *The Free Press* (11 January 1902) p3
'Strange Find On Dead Child's Grave' *Weekly Dispatch* (Sunday 16 March) p1
'Desecration of Grave' *Weekly Dispatch* (16 March 1902)

9.A PLETHORA OF COURT HEARINGS.
'Prisoner Again Before The Magistrates.' *Maidstone & Kentish Journal* (16 January 1902) p7
'The Murder. Magisterial Proceedings.' *The Free Press* (8 March 1902) p3

'Removal of Prisoner' [to Maidstone prison secretly] *The Courier* (17 January 1902) p7

'Saturday's magisterial Hearing' *Sussex Agricultural Express* (21 January 1902) p4

'The adjourned Coroners Inquiry' *The Local journal* (Tuesday 28 January1902) p2

'Assizes Trial' *Maidstone Journal & Kentish Advertiser* (27 February 1902) p6/8

'The Sentence' *Maidstone Journal & Kentish Advertiser* (27 February 1902) p8

'The Trial of Apted' *Kent Times and Chronicle* (1 March) p6

10.THE PHANTOM LETTER WRITER.

'Extraordinary Anonymous Letters. Is the Author a lunatic.' *Kent & Sussex Courier* (17 January 1902) p4

'Tonbridge Murder Sequel. Arrest of Supposed Letter Writer.' *Gravesend and Northfleet Standard* (22 March 1902) p2

'The Southborough Threatening Letters.' *Kent & Sussex Courier* (21 March 1902) pp7-8

11.HAROLD FACES HIS DESTINY.

'Apted execution' *Tonbridge Free Press* (22 March 1902) p3

'Apted's last letters' *Reynolds Newspapers* (25 March 1902) p3

'At the Gaol Gates' *Tonbridge Free Press* (22 March 1902) p3

12.HAROLD SUFFERS HIS FATE.

'The Shadow of the Scaffold' *The Referee* (23 March 1902) p11

'Two executions' *Evening Express* (Tuesday 18 March 1902)

13.THE MYSTERY OF THE ALLEGED CONFESSION .

'Apted Executed. Scene at Gaol, Letter to editor *The Free Press* (22 March 1902) p3

'Rumoured Confession by Murderer' *Maidstone Journal* (27 February 1902) p8

'The Culprits Alleged Confession' *Whitstable and Herne Bay Herald* (8 March 1902) p7

14.AFTERWORD.

Letter commending Styles, Edwin Fowle and detectives. *Kentish Express* (Saturday 8 March) p7
'The O'Rourke Family' *Kent & Sussex Courier* (17 January 1902) p7
'The O'Rourke Fund' *Kent and Sussex Courier* (24 January 1902) p7

15.EDWIN FOWLE BIOGRAPHY
'Late Mr E Fowle. Family's Long Association with Police,' *Sevenoaks Chronicle & Kentish Advertiser* (8 December 1944) p1
The Kent Police Centenary Kent 1857-1957 Published June 1957 by Kent Police. p63 Out of print.

Further Reading
The Kent Police Centenary 1857-1957 Published June 1957 by Kent Police. Out of print.
Prevention, Detection and Keepers of the Peace, Pam Mills, 978-1999813215 Mr Books 2022.
Kent Murder & Mayhem, Roy Ingleton, Pen & Sword Books 2008
Becoming a Police Detective in Victorian and Edwardian London, Haia Shpayer-Makov 31Jan 2007
*

Printed in Great Britain
by Amazon

41923354R00106